Spirituality 101–601 and Beyond

Spirituality 101–601 and Beyond

SHAMARÉ

HEAVEN ON EARTH

© Copyright 2018 Shamaré

Shamaré asserts his moral right to be identified as the author of this work.

All rights reserved. No part of this publication may be produced or transmitted in any form or by any means, electronic or mechanical, including photocopying, recording or information storage and retrieval systems, without permission in writing from the copyright holder.

Published by Heaven On Earth

www.shamare.com

A catalogue record for this book is available from the National Library of New Zealand.

Contents

Preface — vii
How This Book Came to Be

Introduction — xv

Spirituality 101 — 1
The Journey Begins

Spirituality 201 — 45
The Truth That Sets You Free

Spirituality 301 — 87
Simplification

Spirituality 401 — 127
You Are Light

Spirituality 501 — 149
Heaven On Earth Awaits

Spirituality 601 — 177
You Are the True Cause and Effect

Spirituality Epilogue — 195

Spirituality Dictionary — 209

Spirituality and Healing — 253

About the Author — 299

Preface

How This Book Came to Be

Between 2011 and 2013, these Spirituality Notes were released progressively to many friends around the earth.

During this time period, after each chapter was completed and roughly edited, the new pages were emailed to the 'Friends List'. This original list grew into several lists over time, as more asked to receive it. It continues to grow. Hence the book.

After a period of time, I was inwardly prompted progressively to write another chapter, and the distribution process was repeated. It was not urgent to get it done.

There was no book design, no pre-work for the chapters, nor planning for the words written. In other words, this book was not designed or planned consciously. Even when writing, I never tried to think of what to say or even knew what was being written until the instant the keys were struck. The narrative was playing in my mind as I typed, but not ahead of the typing. It flowed from a deeper part of self.

After a chapter was typed up, I would read it and marvel at what was there, staring back at me from the computer screen.

Most times when I was prompted to write, I would sit blank in front of the computer and wait, and then it would flow out. I could pause or do something else and then come back and the flow would pick up again from where it was stopped.

Sometimes during typing, the flow would stop and the mind would go blank again. I would wait, and then it would start again after a short pause.

This is how all my writings are on any spiritual discussion. No planning, no design, no pre-thought of the names, topics, subject, or words. Just sit down and start typing when the flow starts.

From month to month or chapter to chapter, I would forget what had been written previously, but I was certain the next chapter would knit tightly with the last and lead to a progressive flow of enlightening energy, ideas, and words.

I did not know where it was going, although sometimes I would get a preview of what would be written months in advance, and I would include a short snippet on the preview information in the current chapter, as a heads-up for the readers of what was coming later.

I never knew how that preview information would slot into the chapters months ahead, but they always did smoothly.

It was a case of allow, trust, and embrace.

There was a time gap of about one to two months between each chapter, which was to allow each reader the opportunity to read the new material several times, assess this, and finally let it be bedded down in each of their minds.

For some in the group, as they integrated each chapter's theme, their Spiritual Life started to open and evolve, and Mind Healing started and progressed throughout the publishing period.

After all the chapters were completed, there was a pause in the writing prompting. After some time, inner prompting again came; encouragement came to convert the chapters into a book, to allow for a bigger audience so that many others can benefit.

The original work was reopened and edited and expanded to make it more readable for first-time spiritual readers. The original notes were cryptic.

The name of the book, 'Spirituality 101–601 and Beyond', was there as a thought from the beginning, and it is to signify that the information is a metaphor for a university course.

However, I did not know it would be a book. I just had the title. I thought it was like all the other writings over the years, just for myself and my close friends around the world who were interested in healing.

In this Spiritual course, which is to be applied to your life unfolding, the intellectual mind is used to understand the words and ideas, but fundamentally the Real Mind is the instrument that brings a progressive awakening and healing.

Some people like to refer to this as the awakening of 'the heart of man'. 'The heart of man' is a metaphor for the 'Soul and Spiritual Real Mind' combination. It seems to be a stronger seat of motivation than the intellectual mind.

The original chapter names are maintained in the book.

When reading the book for the first time, you will find it beneficial to go through the chapters linearly, as each chapter contains progressively building themes and concepts that become keys to entering a Spiritual Life by Healing the Mind.

Therefore, the purpose of this book is to assist anyone who wants to awaken and return to Joy and Peace of Mind with awareness of Love flowing to them and through them. This is a full Spiritual Life.

This is not a religious book, but it does contain references to some religious material in the form of correction and expansion.

Most of the important so-called 'Sacred Secrets' are revealed, which if you are religiously inclined may reshape your thinking dramatically.

By the way, you all know the information you will read in this book, even if you swear you have not seen it before.

By the end of the book, you may very well agree, 'I do know'.

Much of the information flows as a consolidation of my spiritual life experience in this incarnation—from a small child of three having its first remembered spiritual experience, through many endeavours and experiences to gain knowing, culminating in finally linking up with Jeshua Ben Joseph's ACIM ('A Course in Miracles') and his 'Way of the Heart' audio channellings, and other Jeshua channellings that ran for many years.

Jeshua and his friends lent a hand also in this writing, at various points directly and indirectly, consciously and unconsciously.

By the way, the reason you may not seem to know this information at present is that each soul in human incarnation creates quite an elaborate illusional identified ego self, which blanks off their conscious connection to their true spiritual self.

The book's objective, then, is to offer tools and information that if used and applied will allow each reader progressively to start to identify with True Self again inside Reality, and to de-couple or un-identify with the created ego-self inside a creation.

And a letting go of the many things that only seemed important at some point along the way starts to take place and accelerates as awakening comes to mind.

The spiritual journey home is activated by you correcting your mind. There is no magic or ritual required, no beliefs, no rules, and hence it brings to each searcher great freedom.

By the end of the book, if you have applied what you have read, you may very well be walking in a very different mental state. You will not be the same. Most things will seem different and easier, sweeter, less serious, more fun, and your real Joy and a quiet Peaceful Mind may well be present continually.

You also may feel empty inside, as most fear, guilt, and judgment will have ceased or at least eased off.

As a last point, none of this information you read in the book is to be assigned as a serious thing in your mind. The purpose of the words is to allow you to discover the truth for yourself in yourself, and then to progressively heal yourself, with yourself, in a light and loving environment.

This is light itself that is coming to you, your light, so lighten up and enjoy the development of your great power and freedom that is yours always.

So to set the stage as it were, let us move into our mind healing discussion quickly and get to the heart of all these matters early.

Why waste time? There is an incarnated life to live, and living it in Joy and with Peace of Mind, plus with Love flowing to you and through you, not from a source separate from you but from the very depth of you, is a delight to be had by all.

Love to you all

Shamaré—The Guardian, the Protector, the Door Keeper, and the Gate Keeper

Introduction

The word *Spirituality* has taken on broad meanings over the many years humans have been discussing this subject.

For many, the word *spirituality* is used to wrap themselves in an assumed identity. 'We are a people with spirituality, a nation with spirituality, a culture with spirituality, a race or ethnic group with spirituality, a religion with spirituality'.

This is often used to delineate them from those of other groupings, who they may say or feel have less or little or no spirituality.

Spirituality in ego mind can be used as a term to separate one from another.

It can therefore be used as a term to create human levels or degrees of being special or exclusive in some way.

When anyone uses the word Spirituality in these contexts, they are creating dualities. Possibly using the duality to make themselves seem better or different, possibly distinct in some way.

You will find as you read this book that Ego

dualities regarding spirituality are only illusions and never true.

In truth, where we all exist at all times, all are spiritual in nature primarily, fundamentally or first. So no division is possible. All are inclusive in the spiritual domain, with no separation or specialness.

The All truly only exist in this one spiritual domain. No one can leave this domain or ever has.

Spirituality is inherent with this fundamental spiritual nature, and this spirituality can be projected into a created or virtual domain, such as a human society, or not. It is a choice. However, be aware that if spirituality is expressed through ego mind into that domain, that spirituality is only a mimic creation, not a reality.

Some, while playing human being, even disown their own true spirit nature and say this is nonsense to say 'We are spirit with spirituality', saying or substituting instead the thought, 'We are fundamentally animals with intelligence'.

This is never true or possible, of course, as animals are creations also, even so for human bodies. Spirit is not a creation, it is a fundamental energy residing in the Reality.

So the true nature for all things is spirit. It is the

fundamental. All created so-called life, all matter, all things originate in and from spirit. This is even true for three-dimensional space and time universes, as they are creations also.

It can be no other way, as true life only exists in spirit. Life may be seemingly imbued into created things such as bodies, but if that spirit energy is removed, then immediately those forms cease to seem to live, and they become inanimate. Therefore it is spirit that causes animation.

So the purpose of this book is to re-introduce spirit to those who may have forgotten or lost connection with spirit (difficult to do entirely), or have been too busy to notice or maybe are plainly misled by their ego, intellect, perceptions, and beliefs.

And with that process and progress of re-introduction of spirit self to self, expose facets of the nature of spirituality. Inside this process, over some time, the mind will start to heal itself of this mis-perception of not being fundamentally spirit and many other follow-on mis-perceptions.

This process of mental healing will continue for some time. Mental healing is the clearing out of the mind of the many mis-perceptions, mis-understandings, and beliefs, these usually being wrapped inside many guilts, judgments, and fears that shape life as a human being.

Inside this mental healing process, a new You arises, it would seem. However, it is the Real You that arises; the other you, the ego you, is just a construct, a creation, a mental projection, a mis-understanding or a mis-perception, born from seemingly losing spirituality.

For those who are in a religion with a culture and many belief patterns, this information may be a breath of fresh air for you, freeing you from the many human mis-understandings, mis-perceptions, and behavioural limits proposed inside that religion, culture, or belief system, and slowly setting you free from the many books that proscribe how it all is to be.

Inside these types of systems, there are many proscribed ways of being or behaving or adhering to beliefs, and these are often required and are equated to being spiritual or having spirituality. Never true.

Of course there are many religions, not just the ones that call themselves such, religions even extending into the intellectual, philosophical, scientific, and political.

So this does mean that we will look at the many

facets of life as a human being and examine Spirituality in relation to this.

Many of you may be thinking, 'Spirit and spirituality, it is something I know little about, it may be interesting to have a look. I have read the books of this world but can't find what I really need in them. I need a little more meat, please'.

Excellent. Do enjoy the words; but more importantly, enjoy yourself as you join your mis-perceived identity back to who you truly are, spirit, having projected out of that realm and incarnated on a created planet somewhere, just for the experience to be and play human. To know flesh and with it all the interesting dualities, beliefs, perceptions that are bandied about in this realm.

Even in these created realms where it is seemingly possible to lose connection with true identity and develop an alter ego identification, you are safe at all times. You truly can never lose your True Self or identity. You may try as hard as you can, by burying yourself in the new ego identity as a human being, but at some point you will want to come back home. Sort of like going for a holiday, getting lost in all the fun but eventually knowing that getting on the plane and flying home again is required and essential.

And my dear friends, here is the nub. You never did leave home; it was an elaborate hoax, a grand illusion you created for yourself, to make it seem you had left, but always you are at home, you are just dreaming of holidays and experiences and making new identities by mental projection.

None of this human realm is our true Reality. It is only creation, a play thing, and can pass away (and usually does) when bodies cease to function further, at so-called death.

You, however, always remain in Reality, as you were originally formed as spirit, unchanged, unchangeable, and unchanging forever.

And if this seems odd or confusing, keep reading, as you will find out how to re-introduce yourself to your True Self and know again.

In the back of your mind, you may have thoughts of this in some way.

You can learn how to live with love flowing to you and through you at all times, with the gift of a peaceful mind and having great joy beyond human understanding.

You will learn to love yourself fully and appreciate all the gifts inside of you. And there are many, way beyond your perception at present.

You will discover only Love is Real, and all other mental contrivances that humans live and play with—such as fears, judgments, and guilts—are only temporary and unreal creations, formed and held in place with a thought or two for a while, only to disappear when the creator (possibly you) lets them go and they dissolve away, and are forgotten. As a dream is forgotten.

This is what this book is about. Forgetting your dream and coming home in awareness.

It is a slow introduction to your True Self, the Spiritual you, brimming with Spirituality. Each chapter from *Spirituality 101–601 and Beyond* is a step closer.

Not all questions will be answered. However, the tools will be given to allow you to answer each and every question you have ever had about yourself and your existence.

You will change identities and viewpoints several times along the way and wonder when will this metamorphosis ever stop.

Enjoy all these changes, as you slowly wander down your own personal pathway to meet yourself.

I look forward to meeting you one of these days also.

Love to you all

Shamaré—The Guardian, the Protector, the Door Keeper, and the Gate Keeper

Spirituality 101

The Journey Begins

In all cases, throughout the book, the part of you that I am primarily directing the communication to is the part that is best described in this short statement:

We >>> that are in this incarnation are called Human Beings.

Consider these words.

We are Being >>> Human, is another way to say it.

Ask yourself this question:

If you weren't Being >>> Human and there was no body present to play in

What would be there, as you?

This is the piece I am communicating with and always do.

This part of you is always present and is actually the only thing that truly exists.

Everything else is a self-construct, a creation.

The human body, with ears and vocal cords which seem to do the communications in this domain, are only apparatus for the True Self that is remotely driving or running the human body in another domain.

This True Self always lives in that other domain (Reality), and it is not a Creation, as a body is.

This True Self is Spirit in nature, or Intelligent Energy.

Hence Spirituality is about that True Self and that Energy that Spirit resides in. Nothing else.

You will discover that this Resident Energy is the one thing that heals all things and brings Joy and Peace of Mind.

A little definition for you, just in case you are wondering…

A Soul is Spirit that is in individuated experience. This is the so-called 'Individuated You'.

And so, we begin our journey.

I have contemplated many lives over many years, including my own, and the one thing that seems to arise over and over again, sprinkled through all lives now and all other times, epochs, histories, cultures, societies, and groupings, is a collective human desire—even more than a desire, a begging or a pleading, and in many cases, a crying out. Some bend their knees many times in a life and pray, many climb mountains to seek gurus and teachers, many join religious and philosophical groups, and after all this searching and scurrying around, this quest still remains as an unanswered desire in most people's lives.

'Please help us find and master these one or two things and we will be OK, and be able to live life here, Being as Humans.

We desire the secrets to find True Joy and Peace of Mind in our incarnated lives.

We desire to be surrounded by Love!'

Throughout so-called life being human, most souls have Joy, Peace, and Love coming in and out of their mind experience, but for the many, to hold these states for long periods of time seems elusive and difficult.

The reason for the loss of Joy and Peace of Mind is that we often still find ourselves being re-active, frightened, upset, hurt, judgmental, being right, being wrong, guilty, overwhelmed, confused, perplexed, and many other emotions and we drive

Joy and Peace of Mind out the door of our mind, and Love seems to stop flowing when experiencing these emotional upheavals.

And also, when we are in the midst of these self-made emotional dramas, which in fact is the time to heal them and they are therefore grand opportunities, we don't seem to have the ability, in that moment of emotion, to bring focus back into the mind and move into healing of our minds.

Often the emotion or drama just seems to run away on us and we lose sight of Love, and with it, Joy and Peace of Mind leave the scene.

And then later, when we are recovered, seemingly sane again, we kick ourselves all over the place saying 'what is wrong with me', or 'what an idiot' or worse.

We all know that one very well!

Therefore, to heal the mind, to continually sit inside Joy and Peace of Mind with Love flowing to you and through you, from the depth of you, requires the development of a New Viewpoint.

Old Viewpoints, ego self-identification viewpoints, do not bring Joy, Peace of Mind with Love flowing to you and through you, from the depth of you.

It is quite clear that if Old Viewpoints did work, the

world would be in Joy and have Peace of Mind by now. Love would surround us all, after all this time.

This book is about how to develop this New Viewpoint.

Viewpoint is the place in your mind where you sit, where you experience and see life.

Where is your place and what is your view?

What viewpoint are you sitting on and viewing life from?

Is it serving you well?

You are not stuck with this old, limiting viewpoint.

You can change this viewpoint, and miracles will seemingly occur.

And so we move to the discovery and building of a New Viewpoint.

By the way, there is only one thing that does heal the mind to allow the development of this New Viewpoint, and it is Love flowing to you and through you, not from a source apart from you, but from a source in the depth of you.

Hold that thought for a few moments and reflect.

And so this book is how to develop this New

Viewpoint by opening of Self to this Love that resides in you. Not somewhere else. This Love as it flows stronger and stronger will then heal the mind of the many mis-perceptions and errors that the Old Viewpoint holds.

Nothing else other than Love flowing to you and through you works, nothing—nothing.

There are no human contrivances or teachings that will heal your mind, other than Love. Self-Love.

You will discover that this Love, which is not human love, flows endlessly and is to become our recognised and welcomed new life energy for all healing and with its welcome, the bringing of Joy and Peace of Mind.

And some of the things this Flowing Love allows you to achieve are:

Love allows all things

Love trusts all things

Love embraces all things

Love trans-forms all things

Love trans-cends all things

Love trans-mutes all things

Love becomes all things.

Imagine having these abilities.

Make this little Love Declaration your mantra, say it to yourself, say it to others, sing it in the shower, skip to it when moving around, go to sleep in it, bathe yourself in it.

And even right now, you may not be aware of this, but fundamentally you are just Love. You were born from Love itself, you are the conduit of this Love, and as you read and change your Viewpoint, you are returning to realise, you are the ambassador for Love.

We will examine this Declaration about Love in more detail as we progress.

Of course, we are not talking about human love here, we are talking about the Universal Unconditional Love, as the energy that flows through all things, sustaining them.

This is the same energy that birthed all things.

And so with that short introduction, we enter into the body of our first chapter, Spirituality 101.

Yes, the beginning of a little course. Have fun with

it; there is no professor to mark your grade. You can even skip class if you like and come back for another session at another time. You decide about this course.

Spirituality 101 is very simple, and it is the introduction of how to start capturing the drama mind moments that arise for you and then running the Love Mantra across the drama right then and there, in present time, to heal your mind of this mis-perceived re-active energy.

or

If you miss the emotional drama moment, to learn forgiveness of self for not catching that moment, and then falling into the healing of the mind in a loving, gentle way after the event and by running the same Love Mantra.

And it is this simple, as you will see.

By the way, we do not make this Universal Love. Love just is, our family inheritance, it is there always and you just need to open yourself to its flow from the depth of you. It is free, as a gift to all life.

It flows through the doors and windows of your life continually and even through the cracks if you are trying to hide from it, maybe in a steel boxed existence.

It is what makes and sustains all things now and forever.

You may like to know that this is the only true energy that exists. It is the fundamental energy.

Here is something to consider about Fear and Love.

Fear is just trans-muted Love, nothing else, so how dangerous can fear be?

Trans-muted means you have mutated Love to fear. It is a mutant energy. You are that clever and powerful and go through this process many times each day.

You just wanted to try your power out, that is the power to create what you want to be and feel, and you got hooked on it and are mentally diverted with the effects of this power, your power.

I am sure you are aware of the two main states of mind that predominantly seem to exist.

Let us look at this more closely.

As your life flows and you are experiencing, and if you are sitting in True Mind, that is in Reality, these are the mental and emotional attributes experienced.

Joy, Peace of Mind, and Love flowing to and

through you, from the depth of you. The default state.

We all experience this. You do not need to be taught this, it is fundamental.

Watch a child at play!

Now at any moment that you find any of these attributes sliding away, the loss of Joy and Peace of Mind, and no Love flowing, what will arise to replace them, are forms of

Fear, Guilt, and Judgment.

A trans-mutation is taking place in the mind, and you are making it happen.

You are creating it all; no one else is.

Subcategories can be anger, projection, depression, resentment, being lost for words, feeling violated or victimized, etc.—you know, we all know this.

What is making these trans-mutations?

A fearful, guilty, and judgmental Viewpoint in the mind. A mis-perception of how it really is.

This is what the Ego mind is. That stuff—it is unrelenting and seems vicious and insane, hence this state is often referred to as darkness or a dark period in a life.

However, it is all actually an illusion outside Reality, only a construct, created by no one else but yourself.

It doesn't really exist. It is un-Real (not from Reality).

The creation can go away at the wave of your mental magic wand, and it will stop existing, ceasing to be present. This does mean you can control your mental creations, make them and unmake them at any time you desire.

However, you can never remove Reality with your mental magic wand. It is always there, solid, a rock to rest on, to build on.

So mark these two distinct points as pivotal information for yourself.

Therefore, Reality is, in truth, where you reside mentally always.

However, you sitting in Reality can create for yourself virtual mental creations and move inside these and experience these mental creations virtually. If you live inside them too long, you will forget about Reality as your true home, and you have done just that. Forgotten about Reality.

The journey home therefore is to re-discover Reality as mental home and drop creations of virtuality as mental home.

So mark these extra two pieces of information also as fundamental building blocks of new understanding for yourself.

Building blocks for the New Viewpoint.

This also means, then, that this journey is very personal.

If you are really honest, you know deep down that there is nothing outside yourself making you re-act or trans-mute Love and that you have created every last feeling and response that you find so difficult to live with.

You may think in an emotional time that they, over there, are causing it or that particular circumstance is driving you to this mental state.

But no, always and forever you are choosing and deciding how it is mentally for you.

Hence the afterwards, the kicking and the gnashing of teeth, the oops guilt feeling, the self and external judgments, the depression, the anger, the projections at others, etc.

Sometimes in these moments of mental slide

there is a fear that arises in some: I may not get over this, and then what? Am I doomed to be like this forever??

And hence the waving of the figurative collective human arm in the air throughout its history, seeking attention from someone, anyone, please, to lead us to a better way to live life as human beings, with Joy, Peace of Mind, and Love surrounding us.

It is only reasonable! Yes!!

You may have tried many avenues to find mind healing, to return to Joy and Peace of Mind with Love flowing to you and through you, from the depth of you.

Be assured, all those efforts are now all stepping stones to your final arrival back home.

Hence the reason you are casting your human jelly eyes across these symbols of words, deciding and seeing if this information and new way may be for you. Each person will decide what works for them. There are many roads leading home, with only one path to the final door.

And you are actually already Home. (More on this later.) You will discover it can be no other way.

That titbit is just to add a little sweetener and

certainty to your new venture into healing the mind and journeying mentally.

So the demarcations between Reality and Ego are very clear, black and white.

By the way, for those who are numbed out from all of this emotion and drama in their life, this continual trans-mutation of Love to fear in their lives, and now are living the quiet life, the shut-down life, you are also experiencing the ego dark side.

The reason this can be said is clear. In a shut-down, passive existence, there is no real Joy or Peace of Mind, and you will not be feeling Love flowing to you and through you, from the depth of you. The seeming Peace may just be numbness or withdrawal and denial. A cutting off of some or most communication and experience. So no escape artists please—take full responsibility for every thought, word, and action from now on.

You are in for quite a ride to heal your mind, many ups and downs, so hold on. However, it is as exhilarating as a real horse ride and you create it all.

So now let's discuss the slide out of Joy and Peace

and the seeming turning off of Love flowing to you and through you, from the depth of you.

This is the nub of this discussion in *Spirituality 101—The Journey Begins*.

Everyone who has had the experience of the slide from Joy and Peace of Mind, with Love seemingly ceasing to flow, has run into these sorts of thoughts at some point.

Maybe you thought, 'I just got so overwhelmed with the moment and the emotions flowed, I was lost for words or ideas and even thoughts, I became lost inside the mind maelstrom and I forgot my mantra on Love healing all things'.

or

Maybe you have never known there was a way to heal all this re-activity, and you just had episodes in life where it was difficult, with suffering.

If you have not been able to heal these moments of mental re-activities, you most assuredly have reverse played the Love Mantra, with the Ego mind running the drama show many, many times.

Does it run something like this?

I did not allow the moment to flow, I wanted to

turn it all off, and I even begged the other person, 'let's not go there'.

I did not trust that I brought this moment to myself. I am nice and gentle. It had to be them over there. I was frightened; I thought I was going to be overwhelmed.

I could not embrace the painful drama feelings; the fear was too great, and it was definitely not my friend. I only embrace friends. I became as a child again.

I got trans-formed, but backwards. There was no Love flowing to reverse this; I lost it. I lost the Love.

I actually didn't trans-cend: I sank, I drowned, I floundered.

I trans-muted to something I don't like, and I said things I wouldn't normally say. My Ego mind turned me into a projecting monster or a wimp.

There was little Love around inside that moment.

OK. Well done—we have all been there, in varying degrees.

Some people call this your personality or your personal traits. Some say it is part of your nature to be like this.

Really?!

Whatever—a pat on the back for being so good at this procedure and drill. It is probably a repeating pattern of a mental habit.

It seems to happen almost automatically, doesn't it?

See, it is just that: a procedure and a drill that comes from somewhere, an old habit from somewhere.

You do create all your realities—only you—smile—ah, yes—the nub of the discussion.

So with this understanding of your self-creations, it also does mean you can self-create a new outcome for any moment. It is just that simple.

If you are that good at going down the sliding pathway to emotion and drama using ego and creating an insane moment, you can also take a new pathway to healing to return to Joy and Peace with Love flowing to you and through you, from the depth of you once again.

It will get easier.

It is a choice—your choice. Ah yes, the New Viewpoint!

There are two requirements to trap all moments in a very deliberate way to allow for your new outcome, the way you want it.

Courage and Vigilance.

And by the way, I am not necessarily talking about winning arguments or being right or those sorts of things.

I am saying to stay inside the framework of True Reality under any circumstance. That is, inside the energy of Joy and Peace of Mind, with Love flowing to you and through you, from the depth of you. Your natural state, yes.

There are four stepping stones to process while sitting inside these two qualities of Courage and Vigilance.

Desire—Intention—Allowance—Surrender

These speak for themselves, with Allowance being the critical one to reach as quickly as possible.

You must reach a point of mental simplicity and openness to allow the process of Love flowing to you and through, from the depth of you, to do its work of healing your mind.

That means not turning off feelings, but as they

arise, emote, watch and observe, become the Watcher, the Observer. Feel it all.

Start practising being the Watcher of your mind at work; become the Observer of Self.

To get started, you can practise this when you are not emoting strongly.

Stop and say, 'I am observing my mind, I am happy, I am a little restless', or whatever is observed. Expand this observation. Do it regularly: monitor your mind's state.

And then later, after a little practise, step into the real arena and watch your mind trans-form from Love to Fear and then catch this mental switch.

This is vigilance and it does take courage to catch the switch.

You may not be able to hold the Watcher state for too long at the beginning when emoting strongly, but just keep practising until you can be this, the observer of self, in creation.

Here are some tips on managing these situations when interacting with other people and to bring teaching to yourself at the same time. When you enter into a moment that seems difficult with another person and you feel the mental slide from Joy and Peace coming on, start a dialogue about it with the other person. They (and you) may find this odd, but do not worry: it is you that is important here.

Say something like this:

'You know, I am practising watching my mental state, so as to stay in a Joyful and Peaceful state of mind. And when you said that to me, I realised something was triggered inside my mind for me to look at. You just touch a mental re-active button for me; thank you for doing this. Can we keep talking now and see if these feelings dissipate?'

That would probably blow their socks off, as they are probably wanting to project at you or maybe argue, but I would say if you can become this simplistic, this transparent, and this self-responsible, you have definitely started to turn on the Love Mantra.

You allowed, trusted, embraced, and started the process of trans-forming the fear and trans-cending the mountain of energy and possibly even trans-muted the drama experience from fear to Love.

You will know you have done this only if the mental and emotional heat on it dissipates and your mind clears.

If it doesn't, it is OK. You are in the game now, you are in the process. You have entered yourself into the process of Self Love and self-healing.

A simple change of Viewpoint and mental behaviour like this, and in one instant of mental transparency and Love of Self, you will have changed your life forever.

A pat on the back—a different mental habit is arising, and an old habit is passing away.

A New Viewpoint is starting to be bedded down into place in your being.

I am no longer victim. I am feeling freer now.

You will know if you have trans-muted the fear because there they are back again, your three friends: Joy, Peace of Mind, with Love flowing to you and through you, from the very depth of you.

Now when you get very good at this stuff, and you will, you may find one day that the feelings don't dissipate for you. Oops!

However, you have struck gold if this arises, as you have aroused a large body of resistant energy to heal. It has come because you are ready now. Celebrate this moment with great joy. You may not be able to actually heal it in one go at that moment, as you may be overwhelmed. However, you can look back after the rundown of the Love mantra and celebrate a major mental healing that has come to you and by you.

A few tips to manage this moment.

So here you are overwhelmed and the emotions do not seem to want to dissipate. Stay with it. Feel it, let it have its say. Stay trans-parent and open. Do not judge it.

Now say something like this to the other person(s) or self—even maybe through the tears or fears.

'This is a mother lode you have helped bring up for me. You must love me a lot to be able to do this. Just give me a few moments here and I will breathe into this and through this and release it.'

Staying trans-parent, breathe into the feelings, keep them alive.

Allow this intimacy with self and the other person. It will surely allow healing for both of you to come, as the fear has not overwhelmed you entirely. You did not project or blame.

You may say at this moment that you could never do this with your friends, work mates, boss, or even some family members. I venture to say, though, that if and when you do, the word will spread very quickly that you are amazing, and some people will come to you to talk about themselves and their desire to get on the mental healing pathway.

And if you just can't manage this, wait until you have some alone time and regenerate it all, same feelings, same words to the person. In other words, act out the scenario again by yourself. They may even get some healing remotely, as you heal also.

Yes, everyone has to heal, all those you encounter are party to your healing and you to theirs, in some way. Take advantage of this knowing.

If you weren't able to move to healing in the middle of this emotional arising, you may next time or later, and you can go into full mode right there and then. You will feel very powerful when you do this inside the emotional maelstrom, as it is a choice and very deliberately taken.

Another 'by the way'—you do not necessarily have to know what the Cause of the arising energy is in order to heal it.

You do not have to always dissect this supposed human life and all the others you have had to heal. It doesn't matter, and who cares anyway, as long as the resisted energy dissipates and you return to Joy and Peace of Mind, with Love flowing to you and through you, from the very depth of you.

Often the dissection is just more party talk and drama. It can stall your progress also.

Now as a way to reinforce this healing procedure, start doing this if you are able: sharing.

If you did go through an event, a little drama, tell your best friend who is also on a pathway to self-healing about this healing event when you get an opportunity. Open up to them, become transparent allowing great intimacy. Include them in your healing and growth. Emote in front of them again if required. Open to your feelings at all times and watch yourself do it, and release the energy as wholly self-created. Just knowing you are making it all may be enough for it to dissipate.

Tell your friend how you did it—exact words, thoughts, feelings. Re-live it with them and say 'It was amazing, and I am now healed of this' and laugh, really laugh and say 'it is fantastic, it is miraculous', and know that it is, but not really; it is just how powerful and loving you really are, always and forever.

Spirituality 101.

About Forgiveness of Self for the mis–perception in your mental creations.

Now as a closing note:

Practise, practise, practise.

Remember, it took many years of practice to develop your Old Viewpoint. Same for the new one. However, this development of a New Viewpoint is deliberate this time, driven by Self Love.

Also, now as you practise and have success, tell others how to do this.

You may not get the explanation to them correct the first few times, but keep adding to your words, clean up the edges, polish the delivery, and there you are a teacher, a master yourself.

And the last 'by the way': you are really a master already.

This may confuse you, as you may still believe there is much to do!

As you move from body-centric identification (don't you love that) to Spirit-centric identification, you will see this has always been the case.

You actually do not have to learn anything new. You just need to drop the Old Viewpoint, unlearn some old mental habits, mis-perceptions, beliefs, etc., and surrender to the New Viewpoint and allow the new way of being. A surrender into the default you, the real you, the Love you.

In body death, you will find that when you seemingly cross the divide, you will suddenly run slap bang into yourself again, and guess what—you have always been there.

Sort of like the 'Avatar' movie.

Remote podules aren't required, or technology, but you do fire up the avatar body each day and move it around in virtuality having experiences.

You can disconnect at any point, and usually it is when the body is old and worn out.

Some final thoughts.

Remember, if you are running into situations of mental complexity, this is the mental slide also.

Return to simplicity, with a deep breath and a choice, possibly a smile also. Just drop it all and laugh and say 'Caught you!'

Keep it light; you are light.

You are loved always and forever.

It is impossible to be otherwise.

How's the Viewpoint??
Well done.
Love to you all.

Shamaré—The Guardian, the Protector, the Door Keeper, and the Gate Keeper

Addendum

A few more tips

We are not going to move along too fast on this journey until we have the basics settled in the mind.

Here are some expansion notes and thoughts on Spirituality 101 which may be helpful to some.

When 101 was originally released, I asked the guinea pig readers for feedback, and several reported back to me their experiences of watching their mental slides, and some of these observations are quite interesting.

Some actually started catching many of their mental slides and dealing with these re-activities, inside that arising moment.

You also may now be watching and catching. This is quite something to achieve, as it requires your Observer to be present in that re-active moment.

Others said they realised *after* the re-active event that they had missed the mental slide.

You may have your mind saying at some point, 'You missed one!' And you can smile and say 'thank you, yes I did'. And then re-enact the event right then and there and start to heal that particular re-activity.

Some even expressed the view that they are not going to waste time, diving into old habits of being upset about this or that anymore.

If you find yourself entering into this Viewpoint, stop and reconsider.

To heal re-activity, it is not a matter of hardening up or re-resisting the emotions, the dramas, the re-activity, but mental healing is getting over the need to re-act, which is based on some past mis-perception or belief that is held in the mind.

So be careful that you don't shut down on these moments of emotions and never heal and in fact just re-bury old re-activities once again.

To heal, you have to stay with emotions and sit inside them, embrace them, and allow the recognition that you are responsible for the re-activity arising, taking ownership of your emotional and mental state.

I am creating this re-activity. It is mine to do with as I will. I can forgive myself for creating it and release it. I mis-perceived and created in error.

The release is letting go of the mis-perceptions and

beliefs that cause a loss of Peace and Joy and stop the Love flowing to you and through you.

By the way, beliefs are only substitutes for True Reality, and are at best just simple childish illusions, ideas, dreams, insanities of how it really is, a false reality.

In True Reality there are no beliefs required, it just is; hence the burden of holding a whole parcel of beliefs and perceptions, self-definitions, politics, culture, religion, food, wealth or lack of it, health, etc. just drop away as a useless burden, dragged along with a chain from the past.

You mean to say that even some of those things I hold dear to me are going to drop away?

Oh yes, eventually you will realise that they are what they are, and they will be like chaff and just blow away.

Imagine living a life where only Love is Real all the time, and there is only a smile and a Peaceful Mind. This is your birthright (and we are not talking about human birth).

However, you have to decide and choose if this is what you really want, as it is that deep desire which will kick off and sustain the pursuit of true freedom, with Joy and Peace of Mind, with Love flowing to and through you.

What do you really desire??

To see what your desires are, you can try this little project on for size if you like.

Get a piece of paper or maybe even get a little book.

Write down your desires right now. Say just five or six things, then come back to reading.

So you have your short desire list.

Jeshua taught us about doing this little desire list many years ago now, and you will see it becomes a little bit of a joke, really. Because after you are over the desire for the money, the sex, the possessions, the perfect job, the perfect body, the car, the house, the status, and the being liked, etc. (you see it is a little joke) you really just want Joy and Peace of Mind and to be surrounded with Love.

Maybe a few of the others also!

So try it out, maybe for a couple of weeks; write down the list of your desires and watch the list morph as you drop the frivolous and see what it really is that you truly desire.

Because, you see, when you have the big three coming at you (Joy, Peace, and Love) from Reality all day long, what is in the way to having everything you desire?

You are the fundamental creator of your small world here, and as we progress you will see this world expand until you realise you are truly expansive and way beyond this small self.

So some more tips, because don't forget, I have done all of this also, and I was slow and struggled and moaned and groaned and I felt I had to fight everything that came my way for many years.

I am so happy that some of you are making this so easy and doing it lightly, as you know you are light itself and grand creators of your own reality.

Some of those early readers that I see from time to time are truly literally glowing. The Joy is back, their peaceful mind is coming on stream for longer and longer periods of time, and the Power to change is flowing. They are re-discovering their master again.

Now if you aren't at this level yet, here are some more tips.

First, don't compare yourself to anyone. En-Joy

your moments. This is your game; do not let anyone interfere with it.

In 101, we discussed re-activity when being with other people.

It doesn't have to be just when you are with others that you catch the mental slide. It can be when you open a letter from the bank to find the statement saying you have no money left, or a good friend has just left this world behind and you feel alone, or a relationship breaks down, or you fail your exams, lose your job, are told you are ugly or smell nasty, etc. Anything that takes your Joy and Peace away is a mental slide.

So let's work on these types of mental slides now, as the idea of dialoguing with another person may not be you at present. You may be so frightened with human intimacy that you shut down and go for absolutely no real dialogue at all, a numbing out. A submissiveness overcomes you. Anything to keep the Peace.

Maybe saying to someone, 'Look, I am practising to remain in a Peaceful place blah blah blah' is just too much, or you have the thought, 'I am so into automatic that I just can't watch the mental slide taking place. It all happens far too quickly for me to catch at present'.

So let's start with something easier, like watching the news on TV (that got you smiling). Yes, TV news almost always invokes a response; they do it deliberately to get you going, and you may watch over and over again, like getting a fix, until you diet and swear off it. However it still wins every time as all the re-active hooks remain in place in the mind.

(By the way, the mental slide could be just as simple as suddenly feeling depressed even without watching the so-called news. Anything that mentally slides you into no Joy or no Peace.)

So sit and watch TV or your life (it is a big TV), and as the feelings arise, start a quiet internal dialogue with self.

We will work this example with Self as it may be easier. The need for privacy may still be strong at this beginning mind level.

Say something like this.

'Excuse me, Self, I am working on staying Peaceful and in Joy and allowing Love to flow through me, and this TV news is pushing my re-active buttons all over the place. I sit here and I am making judgments on many things, places, people, and events. I would like to take just one of these things and sit in it and work through the healing process on it. Is that OK?'

You are allowed to be a little whacky, you know, make it funny, make it light, make it silly and smile as you go through this.

It is seriousness that locks re-activity in your mind.

OK, so you have your event that got you all steamed up in your mind, that turned on the emotional and re-active juices. Now turn the TV off and sit and imagine and feel everything to do with that event that caused the re-activity to arise, feel it, and feel it, merge with it, let it build and consume you.

Emote. This is you being the creator, the master. You are choosing the response; you are making the response based on a mis-perception that needs healing.

Now ask self as you sit in the middle of this energy, 'Is this energy I am making, is it something I wish to continue in? Does it serve me well?'

Now breathe, because you probably have stopped or become shallow. Diaphragm breathe and get perspective again, and smile and say, 'Self, I am getting perspective, I am lifting out of this mental re-activity, this emotional drama, I am lightening up (and that is true)'.

You are now through. Love allows all things. You did

not turn it off, you felt the judgments, the fear and guilt, etc.

Now Love trusts all things:

Say to self, 'OK self, this a grand opportunity to heal that piece of my mind that is all upset. I have chosen this event to heal a piece of myself, I am trusting this arising event has come to me so I may heal my mind'.

Breathe, keep it all alive, do not turn it off, feel it in the body (Where? Name the location), watch it and marvel at it.

Once you recognise this as self-created, say 'Self, I know I am creating this mental re-activity; however it seems as a mystery to me where does it all come from. I am feeling and watching it; it is amazing. I have done this so many times automatically and thought this was the only way to respond, but now I see there may be another way'. (And smile or chuckle or roar with laughter as it is your own joke with self.)

You are launching the master now in a different way.

You have just slipped across into Love embraces all things.

Say 'Self, I am going to hold this fear as a friend that

I have brought to myself to allow healing with Love. It is my teacher. (And I thought it was my enemy all these years.)'

Sit inside this as your mastery and power come flowing to you.

Say 'I embrace you as friend' and breathe, stay there and sit in it and allow Love to dissolve it away and you will start to feel Joy and mental Peace returning.

This may take time or not.

You are now inside Love trans-forms all things.

You may, as you sit with your eyes closed breathing, have flashes or recollections, or snippets of video and audio from the past where this all originated from, or you may have a deeper dialogue or find it just dissolves.

Every situation is different.

You have now allowed Love to trans-cend the fear, the experience, the thing, and the monster is now become a friend, something that has brought change to your mind.

You will never be the same again. You are a new person and your mastery is returning, via desire, intention, allowance, and now surrender as you move to this new place.

Next the realisation that only Love trans-mutes all unreal created things.

This is a life-changing event, no matter how small or large.

There is no order of magnitude in miracles; all are equal and as useful.

Joy and Peace of Mind with Love flowing to you and through you have returned, and all you did was sit, watch, breathe, allow, trust, embrace, and watch the trans-form (changing form), the up and over of fearful energy trans-cend, the trans-mute (changing from once substance to another or energy from fear to love).

So there is the process. You may not get through all of that in the first go.

Actually you may be surprised at what arises for you in this process.

It may be a resistance to holding the emotion in place. You may find you jump out of the emotion.

Or holding the memory of the event. You drop into

the memory of the event in the past and you find you jump out because of fear, maybe even changing the subject and having to walk away and do something far more 'important' like clean the house or car. Smile.

Or you find you can't embrace the emotional drama moment of healing as a friend. The fear is too great, and you cannot let go. You sit in the emotion, and the memory of creating the original instance of it arises, and fear takes over and you cannot move to embrace and allow Love to do its thing. You may need to return several times to this or get a friend to work with you and hold you in place, to allow Love to de-fuse the fear.

Usually your Love for Self will win, and you will find a way to proceed. You will be very happy in that day.

By the way, you do not have to win every occasion. You can leave some on the shelf for a rainy day. This is not an exam to be passed. It is an unfolding experience, happening for you in the right order.

Or you may find the ego mind will get you into a drift away from what you're doing. You suddenly realise you are off point and day dreaming again or even going to sleep or now snoring away. Ha ha, well done.

Dialogue these little off-subject mental slides and

come back. Use a mini Love Mantra session to dissolve this sabotage pattern and return to the original healing.

Continue on. Each time it will get easier and quicker.

Start at this level if you are truly frightened of people dialogue.

But know this, that the fear of people dialogue also can equally be dissolved away, at any moment when you desire it.

Whatever you decree—is.

The universal energy of Love—which is you, the mother, father, god, source of all that is—will flow into any desire you have and will not disappoint you. It is impossible, even if you decide to be fearful again tomorrow.

Always supporting, always loving, always gentle, always quietly being there, always without judgment.

You are safe always, you are Love always, you are Loved always, you are Loving always, you are Loveable always, you are Always, and you are the one you have been seeking all this time, full of all knowledge and wisdom.

Self Love at any level is the power to a full healing of all things.

If you do not feel this about yourself, there is your doorway to healing; enter into that doorway of a mental slide or self-judgment.

If you feel you are not Loveable, there is your emotional doorway to heal. Slide into that doorway and emote and heal it.

Dialogue, dialogue, with others or self but dialogue.

Do not sit in silence dis-empowered any more.

Decide to move through this stuff. There is a new you waiting for you.

Anything that is not Love in you must come out, and it will.

Ask it to come out. It will come out in the right order.

You see, True Self, sane self, or divine holy self (if you would allow that thought) is just waiting as a servant to do all this miraculous stuff for you.

You are in effect during these sessions just saying to sane self, 'I pass this stuff to you', as you breathe and sit in the energies that arise, and as you watch the love flowing, the healing comes and there is a return to sanity.

So allow **All** to arise in you.

It will come in the right order for you to heal.

Love Trusts that this is the case and Love Allows that to happen. And you are Love itself.

You have woven a great tapestry of illusions, beliefs, and mis-perceptions, and you are now unravelling this.

Watch the unravelling. It seems miraculous at first, and then it becomes your very best friend.

You spend a lot of time with your best friend. You feel good with your best friend.

All of that above work in 101 and 101 Addendum—emotional dramas, fears, guilts, judgments of self, resistances, mutant energies—is working with illusions or the un-real.

As there is no reality in any of this work, it does mean you can do what you like with it.

You created it all and now you can un-create it all, as the game of Re-Integration to the One takes place.

How's the Viewpoint??

Well done.
Love to you all

Shamaré—The Guardian, the Protector, the Door Keeper, and the Gate Keeper

Spirituality 201

The Truth That Sets You Free

Are you now capturing the moment as your mind slides from Joy and Peace to a new focus of fear, guilt, or judgment?

Usually when you do courses at university, year one math, English, physics, etc. are numbered 101, next year it is 201, etc. That explains the numbering some of you may have been wondering about. Yes, a little university course, unlike any other.

So you have finished year one, Course 101, and the 101 Addendum (maybe summer school). You can now see why year one is called the freshman year.

Do you need to sit the exam again or can you pass yourself? You will know.

Are you catching your mind slides regularly and saying to self or anyone else standing there:

'I caught it, just by the tail, but I caught it.'

They may think you are mad, but so what? You are catching them.

Before entering into the next stage, Spirituality 201, a little more re-vision on 101.

Ego mind is that part of your mind that jumps you into the mental slide from Joy and Peace.

Ego represent a concept held in a mind as a truth, of a self that lives inside an illusion, with a definition of being Body in separation from True Self, Spirit.

Ego is formed at quite an early age in an incarnation as a human being, with many critical beliefs, mis-perceptions, and mis-understandings that eventually create proof for self-identification as a body form.

Existing in a fabric of Ego (the world), a young mind quickly gets conditioned to an Ego viewpoint, from seeming innocence to mental complexity in just a few years. With the additional creation of these many concepts and perceptions and beliefs of how it was and should and will be for you, a new you arises as Ego self, self-identified and with all the hard evidence it is all true.

LOL on that if you can!

(Eventually you will, when you drop seriousness and the need to be right.)

And as you can see now, the ego mind creates massive illusions of how it all is and should be, all based on mis-perceptions that are created nowhere except in your mind, from fear, guilt, and judgment, driven by the belief in separation from source.

Ego: The great breeding ground of mis-understandings and mental suffering.

Mis-perceptions lead to the need for beliefs, and with it, the creation of a world, society, systems, institutions, government, laws, cultures, wars, starvation, disease, nations, philosophies, religions, and many -isms and -ologies, to try to control, manipulate, propagandise, and explain what it all is and what it is all for.

The awakening process from this ego illusion/dream is simply this recognition, 'You have been tricking yourself all this time and the joke is really on you. (Jeshua)

Nobody has ever done anything to you, and the world you seem to live in is innocent, and there is nothing outside of you.

That last concept is a little like buying a pair of size twelve hiking boots when you are just learning to crawl. You will grow to fit them, at some point. They may sit on the shelf a few years, but one day you will get them down and try them on, and ahh—they finally fit.

So it is with Spiritual understanding.

We were never born into victimhood, and the body and personality are not you but just a created vehicle for experience in this domain.

The Real You remains as you were originally created to be, Pure Spirit. Unchangeable, unchanging, unchanged forever.

This fundamental truth is the one that sets you free.

Any other concepts will entrap you in dreams. Many other so-called truths have been tried, and oh, the results.

You can play it any way you like in this dream domain. There are few restrictions.

However, there is a curriculum at the end of all experiments, dramas, and illusions that all will have to pass through.

This is an entering into a pathway, a mind healing pathway, and all will pass down this pathway at some point in time, to get home and end the ego game, as it were.

When you are ready, you will step onto this pathway.

As you go down this pathway, the experiences for healing and awakening are made personally for you alone, designed by yourself, for yourself of course.

As who else could make it for you? Who knows you better than your True Self?

So each and every moment you are choosing (even if you think you aren't), your mind response, the re-activity, the drama, the happiness, the celebration, the goings on, as master of your life.

The only antidote to all mis-perception is opening and perceiving and again recognising Love flowing to you and through you, at each and every moment, not from some other source outside of you, but from the very depth of you. It has always been there but you have not noticed it. (Maybe you have but you dismissed it.)

Nothing else heals the mind, nothing else works. Nothing.

After all ego knowledge has been formulated and trialled, the only answer is Love.

The world is starting to realise this now, as more and more start to awaken.

The awakening process is speeding up. There are many fountains running that are watering the minds that are awakening. Fertile minds that are watered will grow in awareness, simplicity, and love, with little need to be right about anything.

It will come as the hundredth monkey syndrome at one point. You may be the monkey that gets the banana out of the jar at the top of cage, and suddenly all those you love dearly will know the process also. They are watching you, you know, even from afar, in the corner of the cage.

Yes, yes, there will be death throes of the old ideas, beliefs, and institutions, as they play out and lose power, and are discarded.

Just watch in amazement the players struggling to win—

Who is right?

Who will have the power? the money? the say? the veto? the food? the land? the freedom?

And all those other old ego concepts. Worn out and exhausted and ready to be discarded. You can start now to discard your share of it.

201 is a jump into more understanding of how to step into the pathway that leads home.

Also in 201 we add another game to play, to gain mastery of the moments and your mind.

You may be wondering, how did this Ego game all get started? This Ego madness or insanity, a runaway world of fear, guilt, and judgment and at present seemingly all at the pinnacle of human so-called knowledge and wonderful achievement. (Smile or LOL.)

It is quite a discussion, and we will cut it short in 201 to get at the nub quickly for you.

In Reality, where we all exist always, never leaving, there is only Love as base energy.

Love is your default setting. Accept it.

Inside this Reality, only Truth exists. Getting that sorted out in your mind is a great starting point.

So inside the only thing that exists—called, naturally, Reality—there are no dualities, no right and wrong, good and bad, only singularity.

The one family all equal and loved, surrounded in the one arising energy at all times—only Love flowing to us and through us, and we are that energy always (except in chosen insane moments with ego mind).

We cannot shake Love off or disown it. You cannot 'so call sin' and have it taken away by some higher power than you.

Imagine that, 'oh you have been such a naughty soul, no more Love for you, this eon or ever'.

So to the story on the arising of this mental fabric, the so-called world.

At some point along the way, a thought arose in the one mind.

(There is only one mind, by the way, and we all share it.)

'What would it be like to live in a world without only Love?'

Where duality is possible, love and no love, to experience this and even both at the same time.

Of course, immediately a creation started to provide this experience, as is always true in all thoughts. Creation starts. Even now. Hence the statement 'Be very careful what you wish for!'

By the way, this thought of, 'What would it be like to live in a world without only love', was before 3rd dimensional space and time had been made/created.

The consequences started by that one thought led to this physical universe being created by us for experience, at all sorts of varying degrees of duality.

Many rooms in the mansion to play in, with many shades of colour, as you could say.

Choose your theatre you want to play in.

Ah, Earth seems interesting.

Ah, Being Humans seem a big game.

Bang and there you are.

It is just moving your mental attention from home to there, very easy when you are a multi-dimensional powerful spirit.

And we might as well say it now to get it out of the way:

All power under heaven and earth has been granted to you from the beginning of all things. So grand freedom is yours and remains even now with the mis-perception of self–identification as a body in time and space. (Jeshua)

One of the consequences of the thought 'What would it be like to live in a world with dualities' was a contraction of consciousness, the beginning of fear and a rising feeling of guilt or self-judgment.

As the experience of this creation expanded, so did the feeling of separation from Source or Love or

God (they are all interchangeable concepts). Jeshua teaches God is a four-letter word.

And so it must be true that you are your own salvation. You have created it all and you can uncreate it all. Hence, no saviours on crosses required, no sacrifices either, and you have not sinned. OMG, I hear! You have journeyed forth many times to experience and now you are awakening and want to return home.

Inside the game, the ego experience, the Concept of Separation brought about all sorts of new thoughts; and from that one original thought there developed a world of thoughts, worlds inside worlds, with varying degrees of concepts and perceptions, levels of density, levels of beliefs, many levels, and layers of complexity.

To play the ultimate game of separation, the physical world came into existence, and just to try it on, creations in the forms of bodies were made and then incarnation as an event was born, metaphysically and physically. (Smile on that one also.)

It became possible to project mental attention from Reality into creation, into a created body and open jelly eyeballs in that robot, and listen with skin membranes that vibrate, and make noises with air that carry meaning via vocal cords etc, all remotely while sitting in the 9th Spiritual dimension as a virtual game, an amazing game. (You may be able to laugh on that.)

So bodies bring separation into focus, because separation seems to be so very true with bodies.

You are over there and I am here, with space between us, it would seem.

I am aware now that I am also vulnerable to you and others. I must learn to protect myself. Fear arising.

With incarnation, there arises forgetfulness of spirit, as the focus on body seems so overwhelmingly real, and ego self-identification develops strongly, masking all that isn't body and not in this creation.

The dream of separation developed deeper as groupings came into existence, tribes, cultures, beliefs, religions, books, and so-called knowledge, until a spirit playing as a human being in the 21st century is quite convinced most of the time they are Bob or Mary here, and it is dreadfully serious, and all the rules must be followed to be successful (except maybe on Saturday night when the rules are thrown out for a little while).

LOL—you know this. Each day as you deliberately choose to put your shoes on, laugh about this notion.

Also contemplate, sit for a moment and see how this fits with you and your understanding of life as an ego, a self-identified Human Being, with forgotten focus as Spirit.

Oops, there we are again with that Viewpoint stuff.

Ah, you can see your viewpoint is Body-Centric. Can you see now why religions developed?

We must get back to God, to Source, back to the simplicity of only Love is Real. We must have done something to be separated, we must have sinned, we must do something to recover ourselves, we must find saviours with the right sacrifice, we must be good and nice, we must follow the rules, we must we must. We will even subjugate ourselves to rulers, and they can decide our outcomes for us.

I really want good to beat evil! (Maybe a chuckle on that one also. Ever had that thought?)

Or become totally over awed and just say, 'Oh f— it, who cares, just live and have fun, for tomorrow we will surely die'.

Or be a denier and say, 'My Ego knowledge tells me

I am OK, I am educated, I do not need a concept of Oneness, the whole thing is a nonsense'.

And so on.

And yet all the while, the small voice of True Self is calling to the dreamer:

'Awaken, child, from the dream! It is only a dream, you have gone nowhere, you are still here. Separation is a dream. Awaken now. *Tap tap.*'

To Awaken, you need do nothing at all. You are safe, you are loved, you are still one with all things, save this one thing, the turning of the attention back to where you really exist and what you are.

A shedding of ego identification. A return to spirit identification rather than body.

That Viewpoint stuff again.

You journeyed forth and went insane for a moment inside illusion, inside a dream, experiencing many things, but now return as the prodigal daughter, back home, awake, to a grand celebration, a homecoming.

And so with that short preamble, the journey truly begins now.

The pathway is set. You are going to return to a place you have never left, a journey of no distance. Jeshua's words.

The curriculum to awaken from the dream of separation is simple, but it must be passed through to arrive at the destination you never left. Jeshua's words.

A paradox, of course. Maybe a fairy godmother could just wave the magic wand and it will end.

Remembering Love is the key, hence the introduction in 101, of Love heals all things.

And in this case, your journey home, the same applies. Love does heal all things.

And why is this true—because only Love is Real, and everything else is only a creation or a fabrication or a virtualisation.

You see how that works. Ponder on this. Sit with it until you can feel that truth.

A return to singularity is just that simple. A return to be at one with the universe—'uni' (one) 'verse' (turning). The one turning, not separated in mind. Anchored home, in Reality.

Once you become aware of Love flowing to you

and through you again, from the depth of you, you are in Reality and are home.

Home is right here or over there, or in 5th dimension, or anywhere else, it is all the same.

Heaven is not a place, it is a state of mind.

Many have ventured into a so-called spiritual pathway, determined to win, to get the prize. They have gone to many teachers, gurus, seminars, pilgrimages, the monastery, read many books, experienced self-sacrificing, self-denial, self-flagellation, all to try and purify themselves.

Some have believed in saviours that died to save them and hoped this would short-circuit the whole thing. Some will meditate endlessly and chant, some even doing good works. The lighting of millions of incenses and candles. Decorating altars and a holy countenance. None of this truly works.

Thank heavens for that, I hear some of you say!

And this is true, because we were never called to suffering or lack of Self Love, to be the victim and in a hopeless state, unrecoverable.

Anyone telling you otherwise is lost themselves in the dream. If they are not teaching only Love is Real, all they want you to take on is a version of their own dream, a new cult (smile). A new victim culture.

Each person awakens to their own call, and this call, of course, comes from Self in Reality, from the very depth of you alone.

There is a piece of us in Reality that is not insane but completely sane, and isn't involved in the dream of separation: that piece knows the way home. It is outside the dream.

This is the energy and knowledge for the untangling of the tapestry of your life/s.

It knows your life'/s tapestry. It watched it being made and can assist in the untangling process so that ego is finally made the subordinate rather than the master, and Freedom, Joy, and Peace of Mind return with awareness of Love flowing to you and through you, from the depth of you.

You have heard of heavenly bliss.

This is the greatest story ever told and you are players in it.

Can you see now why the books talk of 'once upon a time', the wonder, enchantment, beauty, love, and 'they lived happily ever after'?

In 101 we said you are spirit, not body.

In 201, The Journey Home, we can expand this idea.

In Reality, we are all one. Hence loving your neighbour as yourself is always true because they are you; there is no separation.

It is a loving composite Spirit with individuation.

All parts equal, all parts loved, all parts intertwined in Love as the unifying energy.

This composite sane energy is your companion now. Once you start the pathway, the process, the two pieces of self, the sane and insane, you could say, start communication and moving towards one another figuratively. A meeting of minds.

This is why the dialogue was encouraged in 101. Minds talking together to become one again.

Some are already having this communication, as they work on the slide work.

Sane Spirit or True Self will probably by now be working in concert with you, and the dialogue encouraged is just that.

So in closing, here is another little game to play to get closer to Sane Self. It is called:

Flying Left or Flying Right.

We will use these two ideas in this new game.

Ego (that is who you think you are most of the time) has developed an endless parade of strategies, sabotages, or self-deflecting methods to hold itself as king in your life. These ego mind tricks are used to turn the figurative head back on itself over and over again, like the bit in the mouth of a horse, pulling itself around on itself.

We may need a little game to fix this deflection.

An example for you of how to play this game of Flying Left or Flying Right.

Once again someone has said something to you or you have had an experience where your Peace is sliding away, and the ego will always say:

Straighten up and fly left.

Fly straight back into the same old misperceptions, beliefs, thoughts, words, strategies to cope, habits or sabotages, re-activities, emotions once again (to deal with the issue that you have raised in your own mind)—the so-called safe way to be!?

Sometimes the thoughts or even the words can be like this when a Fly Left happens and you find yourself in the suffering game again.

Why does this always happen to me?

Why do I get angry, sad, depressed?

Why does it never seem to work out?

Why can't I win some?

Why do I feel bad about this?

Why am I so afraid?

Why do I limit myself?

Why do I accept this?

Why do I accept abuse?

Why don't I have enough money to live well?

I am a good citizen, pay my taxes, obey the laws, but I don't seem to get anywhere.

Almost always a 'Why' question, a victim question.

So here is the game for you to get out of a victim mindset and to stop flying left.

Rather than saying, 'Straighten up and fly left, back to madness'.

Try instead this:

Straighten up and fly right.

So you enter into the mind game and a moment

arises. The old ego pulls to fly left: notice it, bag it, and acknowledge it.

'I just about flew left. But no, not this time. I am not going to say the same sayings I always do when this happens, I am not going to say that 's—t happens' anymore, I am not going to run and hide and say or think all people (at least all people that are fat or skinny or look like that) are nasty and who needs them anyway. I am not going to leave the room when the shouting starts (that is, the shouting in my mind). I am not going to project out with vocal cords anymore and say some nasty stuff just to feel better—a short fix. I am not going jump up and down like I did as a three year old and have a tantrum, I am not going to get depressed, I am not going to plan revenge. I am not going to take some drugs or drink myself into unconsciousness.'

I am going to say, 'Amazing, I nearly flew left again, but now I am going to open myself to this feeling of fear, in expansion, to healing, to start love flowing to me and through me, from the depth of me, as I move further down the pathway to home'. I will fly right this time.

And sing the old Love mantra inside your mind this time.

Love allows all things, Love trusts all thing, Love

embraces all things, Love trans-forms all things, Love trans-cends all things, Love trans-mutes all things, and finally I will see and feel that Love is all things.

Thank heavens I flew right.

At some point in time, after going through this procedure quite a bit, when all things in the mind are cleared and you can say 'I now see all things are made a new in me': you will pass through the figurative eye of the needle and enter into a place of singularity once again, an ending to the journey home.

Another name is Heaven. Heaven is where Love is always. In a smile, even.

Dualities are gone; when you look out into the world, you will only see Love, and this is not a trick or a denial, it is because all judgment is gone from the mind. Imagine that. That day will come.

The journey back to Reality is now complete, and there is someone waiting for you with outstretched arms, and as you get closer you can see it is—yes, You. You have always been there.

You just journeyed forth in dreams.

This pathway and journey home is for those that

would dare to dream that Heaven can come to Earth.

And there you are, as Heaven itself, Love itself (get that) laughing about how amazing the dream of separation was, but it is fading like all dreams do.

And in truth, it never really happened, just as you say today that the dream last night was not real, it was just a dream and has faded away.

So you leave the dream untouched in any way, hence the reason you can always say without contradiction: You are loved, you are safe always and forever, no matter where you think you are, even if you are dreaming.

Another way to examine this concept of dreaming and returning to 'Only Love is Real' is by examining some earlier information given in the 1960s–70s.

In the book 'A Course in Miracles' by Jeshua, it says in the preface:

What is Real cannot be threatened.

What is Unreal doesn't exist.

Herein lies the Peace of God.

Our only Real Job while awakening from the dream is to sort out what is Real and Un-Real, and then Joy and Peace of Mind will flow in us as naturally as Love.

Joy and Peace of Mind are the by-product of being in singularity. Birthright again. No learning required.

Imagine—and please do this.

Sit that body and imagine: look out of those jelly eyes, and see only Love. Just a few minutes each day. Imagine as Spirit you are doing this. In truth you are anyway.

Add more time each day, until...it is all day. Yes you can.

Bless this world with this Love, your Love. Your Love, by the way, is perfect Love. You don't have grades of Love, so your Love is very powerful. Each time you do this, you heal yourself and of course you are all things, with no separation from anything.

As an aside, you may experience this one day, a merging of yourself with all things, with no separation.

A very holy instant. It all became whole for you. There were no holes in it; it was one.

OK, so go play Flying Right and en-Joy the experiences.

Say to one another when it gets awfully serious, 'Fly right', and laugh together or by yourself, to turn it all back to fun again.

You may need to read this several times to get the concepts. You know it all really, it is just masked at present. It will get clearer and clearer as the illusion slowly fades away.

How's the Viewpoint??
Well done.
Love to you all

Shamaré—The Guardian, the Protector, the Door Keeper, and the Gate Keeper

Addendum

Methods to soothe those moments of arising fear

I have been encouraged to go over with you some of the thoughts and reactions you may encounter in your mind when starting to fly right regularly, then to give some methods or responses to soothe these moments, so fear doesn't arise too much.

Be very gentle with yourself always.

From here on forward, there will be more little pieces of advice or tricks to fill in some gaps to manage the transition for you, just to allow you to create more mental balance as you change.

Because change is come, each moment you evolve your consciousness by dropping a mis-perception, that creates fear, guilt, or a judgment.

You may have not realised this yet, but in almost all cases, it is Ego mind that has drawn you to a Spiritual path.

Ego will do everything to stay king of your life, and if some avenues in your virtual life as a human are not working well or there is a persistent underlying issue that can't be resolved, Ego will start looking at the Spiritual for a solution. First as a method to resolve things.

You may have tried many other things in your life to give it meaning, to be happy and secure, and had various outcomes.

If you get the money sorted, then it may be love relationships or children or friends or just a general unsatisfactory feeling about the world in general, or you may have suspicions about self.

Or maybe the politic isn't solving what you think is an easy thing, or the justice system, or blah blah.

Ego will say, let's look at this thing called Spirituality, often trying religion first (as this is often confused with Spirituality), then moving past that to New Age philosophy (this also is often confused with Spirituality), and finally the pathway home opens up.

This information is not new; it is fundamental and as old as creation itself and has been around since then, hence it is not 'new age'.

Let us look at why and how an ego would move your attention to Spirituality.

Let's look at some possibilities in lives as humans. In some cases it can be this crazy before the pathway opens. I know this. You may have experienced some of this also:

Christianity as a child, knowing early that adults are all messed up. Education focus as a teenager and young adult. Some Buddhist philosophy along the way, maybe a visit to India. Reading the Koran, the Bible, the Indian holy books, hunting for a Guru, some metaphysics, Theosophy, Rosicrucians, Scientology, Avatar, a myriad of new age books while cooking dinner, vegetarianism, supplements galore, drugs, alcohol. Conspiracy theories and UFOs, a short look at the Ananaki, joining one of the many groups who are saving the planet, a little politics, business, trying to find money, many modalities of healing, new friends, a new partner, a new house, a new country, monasteries, retreats and advancements and even meditation to the level of a Zen Master, with Yoga and Pilates on the side. Flights all over the earth, many long treks. Etc., etc. Sound familiar?? And one hundred rebirth sessions. Wow—and you are only forty years old. A super human, doing all of this while having a family and buying a new car and house with vacations. Well done.

Or just simply waking up one morning and saying *life has got so crazy—there has to be a simpler and easier way than this nonsense. I am ready now.*

So you can imagine when the ego makes this decision, this is going to be very interesting, because if ego loses authority to True Mind, it ceases to be master, maybe even losing existence. This can become quite an interesting situation to deal with.

Can you feel the tearing?

How to stop being diverted away from your new arising Self Love and stay the distance?

Remember the discussion very early on in 101 about desire? It is your driving force for you. The desire list, as it is refined, reflects the removal of Ego desire and the replacement with Real Self desires.

So, what do you truly desire now??

And if it is Freedom, Joy and Peace of Mind, Love flowing to you and through you, from the very depth of you, you will make the transition across the gap when you follow these simple steps. (Mind the gap!)

Intention gives the driving force and focus required. In all things, where you place your attention, that is where your value or treasure will be, held in place with desire and intention.

If you need to change something in your life, to put

in place your desire, you have the option to do this. It is a simple choice, even if there seems to be some loss attached to the action of choice. Step into it with intention.

This leads to the next most important step, which is Allowance. Allow this new process you have stepped into to take you over, even if it seems uncomfortable, even as Ego starts jumping.

From now on, consider those things that come up in your life in the form of resistance as opportunities of great Joy. It is the arrival of a mind healing moment that you have ordered up.

Let the thoughts be like this: 'This is so good, I am finding things that seem to be wanting me to fly left. Keep them coming.'

'Aha yes, I see that when I was eight years old I was accused of something I didn't do, and I got scared, and voilà: here I am at thirty-five years old, still being frightened of being accused. I must face this down.'

Stare the fear right in the face, feel it properly, sit in it for some time and then laugh with that master energy that trans-mutes this back to Peace. This will come in time, with practise.

Enter into a life of simplicity and trans-parency—no

secrets, seek no specialness, either for self or with others. Be even-handed.

Open to intimacy—let them look inside you with no blinds or shades pulled down. Become naked.

Let your yes mean yes, with no hidden agendas.

Confess openly to those you know well, all that is going on.

'You know I am feeling a little lonely right now.' A hug might be enough.

Start minimising the editing of your communications; that is, before you say anything, picking it over and deleting the stuff that may upset them all.

Say it as it is, and then if there is some stuff that is a little odd, say, 'Oh my god, did you hear that? Where does this nonsense come from?'

And laugh and laugh, flying right, always flying right.

All the nonsense will eventually just smooth out and go away and you can communicate safely, lovingly, without effort. Say what you mean, don't pull back. If it comes out all inside-out and upside-down, it is again an opportunity to find the cause.

(More on Cause and Effect later in 301.)

If you bury it all again, you will only ever have the effects flowing. The cause will be hidden away in the closet with all the other skeletons. Bring out the closet, open the doors, and have a bone sale or a bone burning.

If there is something you feel you need to do, go do it. If you feel you need to go see someone and fix up something, do it.

If you are in a relationship in which there is lack of respect or even abuse, ask yourself this:

Am I contributing? Am I a lap dog? Do I lose my voice? Am I frightened? Am I missing the point here? Am I afraid of loss? Am I seeing a mirror of myself in all of this?

What can you lose by opening up to all of this? Maybe you can empty the cupboards and sit in quiet and peace again, with no weighing down, no secrets eating you up.

Courage is required. Start a dialogue with the other to get a few things sorted. Ask for a respectful time each day or week when this can happen. If it is not given, then you can ask other questions.

Am I at Peace with this? Can I let more go and allow Joy and Love to flow inside this? Am I the issue here? Am I taking responsibility? Are they taking responsibility too?

And when it becomes very obvious that self-responsibility is lacking from the other, you can part with sovereignty, Joy and Peace intact, wishing the other well with no malice or loss of Joy. This may take some time, with a load of courage.

You decide how long.

Continuing on with some tips.

Also ask yourself, do I project my fear out at others?

Do I use communication to cause guilt in others? Ego communicates in these ways.

As you progress down the path flying right always, these types of behaviours will slowly dissolve away and be replaced with Peace, and then 'Peace beyond human understanding' will flow over you. Ego can't understand this.

I would like to talk about how easy it is to transform.

You may have heard, 'The load is light and the way is easy'. (Jeshua)

Well, how can it be any other way unless you make it so? It is your gig.

These little truths are self-evident, if you place yourself on the other side of the divide.

As Spirit self, this humanity stuff is just a very small point of focus.

In other words, don't sweat the small things, and all things are small things anyway in the overall scheme of things.

So take heart, even when the ego is baulking, and smile your way through it all. You can't smile properly without releasing the fear. Just keep practising the smile until it blossoms, and then let out that large sigh and know it is ended. Then laugh at it all. Feel your freedom.

You can ask your friend also to push and prod that smile out of you if it is hard to find it. Then laugh about that prodding and the love your friend has for you.

Also in 201, the idea was introduced that one thought leads to a world of thoughts, with worlds inside worlds of thought.

You are that series of thoughts in Ego mind. You have customised it to fit your Ego Self-Identification.

And so as you eliminate this and move through the healing of anything that is 'Not Love' in you, you will find yourself going through levels and layers, just like an adventure computer game. Worlds inside worlds of thoughts, with mis-understanding and mis-perception that you have created.

Don't forget, this world is the ultimate virtual reality. We are only mimicking this world in two levels of virtuality, with computer games.

So, as the layers and levels go, you will find yourself saying:

You know I haven't been angry now for months.

You know I don't say all that silly stuff anymore.

I don't seem to get depressed now.

I don't sabotage myself in front of people now.

I can talk to those people now so easily.

You know, mum and dad weren't so bad—I can hug them again.

A little more on mother and father issues. If in fact you are pure Spirit—and I assure you, you are—who really are your mother and father? The human ones did not give you life, but they did make a body for experience.

And you came together through prior arrangements. Look carefully at your family and see what is being mirrored back to you. What is it you do not like? These are the parts of your perceptions to trans-form, trans-cend, and trans-mute.

Continuing on.

I can now let my children grow up without fear, without that burden of control and worry—amazing!

I can talk intimately with my partner and children and family with ease now, phew.

I don't need to keep all those people on Facebook as friends anymore, to seem as if I am popular or happy or a successful human, smile.

A little more on being nice and good: Give it up. It is an ego projection. Allow your life to flow Love; Love is much more nourishing to others than niceness.

I can move on from relationships without loss of Joy. Yea!

I can move into a relationship without loss of Joy and freedom. Wow!

And so on.

Just let it all go. It is all unimportant and Unreal. It is creation based on mis-perception.

Now the day will come when you bang into something that seems very big and ugly, and it will not trans-form or trans-mute. Oops. In cases like these, it is how much investment you have in this ugly thing that decides it stickiness. Deeper layers contain deep things. You will be most surprised what some of these are.

Don't fight. I used to fight them. 'A spiritual warrior always wins.'

No, that is Ego talking.

By fighting, you are making the Unreal, Real. Oh dear!

So feel it all, and slowly over time you will find the path will clear. Trust this, allow this. Surrender to the mystery of the process. It is all OK. Just give it some room and some time.

It doesn't matter.

This is an interesting choice of words: 'It doesn't matter'.

In other words, the fear, the thoughts will not *become matter* and bite you in the bum.

It is only mind; and you are the master of mind always, whether ascending or descending.

Here is a simple method to handle some things that seem sticky when they arise (and they usually do).

Breath is a helpful method to keep from being overawed or frightened by these arising emotions.

Hence yoga, rebirthing, meditation techniques. The ancients knew this much, that breath leads to opening mental doorways. You actually shift domains if you breathe deeply enough.

So in the sticky moments, you will usually find yourself flying left, usually in fear, guilt, and self-judgment, often with shallow breathing.

Catch it, fly right, breathe deeply and rhythmically and move your attention to the feeling in the body. You will then descend into and reach the emotional field. Bathe yourself inside the emotional field. This is the embrace. You will feel the energy field surrounding the emotion. You may see colour in these fields, you may feel heat or cold, it may seem sharp or smooth, heavy or light.

The trick, of course, is to become fully aware at these moments that you are actually supplying energy to the emotional field, keeping the emotion alive, and have done so for many years. This is one of your pets you feed continually. Some seem as monsters. (smile)

As an aside, this is one reason that as people get older, they often gain more pets to fed. They often have so many fears/pets they are feeding energy to, that they are exhausted running around feeding them all.

You, though, as master of the energy and thoughts, can decide and say 'I release the energy feed, I am not going to feed you anymore'; and as the fear/pet slowly fades, you can then invite or open to Light and Love to flow through you again, from the depth of you. The trans-form, the trans-cend, and trans-mutation.

That overwhelmed feeling, that heavy tired feeling, that old bones feelings, will go, and you will enter Peace again. Refreshed, of course.

Each day you will be a new person. You will forget the way you were. Others will comment at some point and even ask what are you doing.

You become a new creation daily, even moment by moment.

Look through your jelly eyes in the robot and see only Love a little more each day.

You will notice this happening as the need for judgment subsides and Joy and Peace are more important.

And in closing, a little for you on God energy, Source energy, Love energy. This energy is closer to you than your own breath. It is less than the width of a thought in distance from you, at each and every moment. The immediacy is palpable. (Jeshua again.) Without this energy flowing, all lights would go out everywhere instantly. Everything (everything) is connected intimately always as one to this source of energy, even in ego minds on a so-called created distant planet where human robots masquerade as Real Separate Entities but are just real separate entities.

A little parody on Jeshua's sayings.

Also re-member—that is, make sure your thought of bringing a past event to you gets a new set of legs (or new 'members') and give it power to move again, to dance for you.

So put new legs on an old memory and it comes alive for you in the present as a re-membrance.

So re-member, a thought carries great power and is faster than the speed of light. In fact, in all creation and all universes, a thought will reach all points or corners at the same time. No time.

Each time you have a Loving thought, each time you trans-form, trans-cend, and trans-mute fear, the whole universe knows this simultaneously, instantly.

You are changing all things as you change, because, again, you are all things, as there is no separation. Nothing else exists.

I know at the moment much of this is as concept, but the day is coming for you to know this, not intellectually, but know as a feeling, as a truth, as a reality that requires no more words or discussion.

It is complete when you are ready to say it is complete.

Now just a last concept for you.

Some in the family may have had so-called death arrive, and it seems to take away a member.

Death is an illusion. The only thing that truly happens is the body/robot ceases to be animated, and the human game for that person is ended.

In Reality, where we only exist, that Spirit soul has just put down the virtual reality game console called 'human life' and walked to the coffee machine for a break.

They are still in the gaming room with you. They can't leave; there is no way to escape, no door.

The feeling you have of separation at a human level is an ego perception trick, a mis-understanding and joke you play on yourself.

Love to you all once again and never forget, we are always together always. Jeshua

(Actually he said 'Never forget I am with you always'. It has to be true, where is there to go to?)

Well done.
Love to you all

Shamaré—The Guardian, the Protector, the Door Keeper, and the Gate Keeper

Spirituality 301

Simplification

As we delve deep into Spirituality, it may come as a surprise that we do not put more knowledge layers on the top, as in ego knowledge, but we simplify down.

So for Spirituality 301, we are going to go deeper into the simplicity of Love, as this is our only True Reality and Freedom.

This of course will remove any tendency for anyone to think they have more knowledge and be more important than others.

Imagine—a scholar of spirituality!! Now that is worth a good laugh. Sort of like a Tom Turkey all puffed up and the tail feathers all nicely arranged, but making strange noises. Smile.

Intellectual knowledge is not where it is at, but the simplicity of being and experiencing is where it is at.

A knowing inside simplicity.

Let's start with a simple word picture.

Unless you become as a little child, you cannot enter into the Kingdom of Heaven—Reality.

An expansion on this by the original spokesperson, this time given in the 1990s, is—

Unless you become as a cat sitting by the refrigerator, you cannot enter in to the kingdom.

A cat just sits, waiting at the fridge, and knows thoroughly that it will get fed. Sometimes not too patiently, mind you.

Your feeding or knowing will come when it is the right time, and it will be real food, not from intellectual learning. Keep Joyful and be patient; knowing will come. The flow will come.

This does sort out the wannabes from the True at Heart, and very quickly.

So if you have got this far and have found simplicity is your thing, a pat on the back. Gold stars are being passed out to the group right now. No champagne yet, though.

Between 201 Addendum and 301, I have had several opportunities to sit for some hours and be with some who are new to opening up and catching the slide and flying right. They all want to heal.

Some I have sat with over emails.

First, thank you for letting me be with you as you discuss your life and your mind and the desire to heal it. It is always so amazing to see this process at work. There is so much commonality in these discussions:

First the suffering, pain, or re-activity in mind

The overwhelm and tendency to fly left, first of all, into victimhood

Then the desire to heal arises

Then the way to achieve healing (the Love Mantra)

How sometimes it seems difficult

Progress seems slow sometimes

Even like a snail

or

I just don't get it yet, it is hard to grasp

So this is why the need for simplicity, to allow all in, not just the clever. Complexity and cleverness have got us to where we are now as human beans.

Unravelling and healing have to be done with a simple Loving Method.

I sit and open myself to what is needed for these Spirituality Notes (now a book), and always the thoughts, ideas, words just come to me in a very simple way. I am given freedom to write as I do, and then sometimes I am asked to edit a little, to make it become simpler or clearer.

If you find it unclear or vague, read again and then if this persists, just leave it, so the understanding can come some other way.

Most often, a perception or a belief is in the way.

This is the ego's mental process of blanking out the beautiful view of the Real mind.

The time between 201 and 301 was no different, and as usual I always write seemingly automatically, without thought or discussion. I do not plan or formulate this work. I do not even know what the next word will be as I write.

In this chapter, I would like to add some external information and share a piece of an email discussion with you, from one of the original reading group members. It could be you writing this and asking for help, an answer.

Statement from one in the group:

> I am flying right quite a lot now and then flying left sometimes and it seems huge? (that is the feelings that arise flying left)

Answer by email:

> Even when flying left, it is OK to stay in the feeling and watch yourself/mind, as observer.

See if you can do this.

In fact, you are not flying left if you do this, unless you go into re-activity and drama and lose connection with self and let it all go automatic.

So feel it all, watch it all, sit with it all, and wait—then become aware and know you are creating it all!

Sit with that knowing until anxiety lessens.

Then start to dissect that awareness, the knowing, as you sit in front of the feeling.

Notice the edges, notice the energy, find the colour, the shape, and the surface of the emotion and energy—is it smooth or sharp, hot or cold, large or small?

All creations have form at one level or another, even emotion.

Then move to asking, 'Have I had this before?' and wait for the re-collection/s, then list off when and if you can see the circumstances.

Then move to seeing how you have participated in the building and creating of this energetic and emotional body, for some type of experience.

It is only a mental ripple. And now move to the point of asking, 'Well, is this an energy I choose to remain in?'

Then decide, and if you choose release, withdraw the energy flowing into the creation by withdrawing your value from it, by saying something like this:

> *I am now choosing to release my creation and to move back to Peace.*
>
> *I see it was only an illusion, something I created. It is not Real. It is not Real, I made it.*
>
> *It did not bring Peace, and I value Peace and Joy now over this mental drama/creation.*

If you find the creation stays or persists, you can expand the words by saying, as you look and watch it:

> *You know I own you! I made you! I feed you, and I have decided now that I choose to free you. I now release you!*

If this is done when you are embracing the re-activity as now a new friend, and not fear, judgment, or guilt, it will dissolve away. Love does this. You allow Love to dissolve it. You withdraw value and stop trans-mutation of Love to the re-activity and allow Love to bring peace again to your mind.

Smile and laugh and say

> *There, I undid what I did. It was fun.*

Acknowledge and say

> *I am that powerful. I can create and I can let my creations fade away.*
>
> *I also now perceive that Reality always remains solid for me.*
>
> *I can now feel and know the difference between my creations and Reality.*

Many teachers would say that after you have healed yourself of that difficult creation, you can create a new creation for yourself that gives purpose, reason, and more meaning to life. We, however, are in the game of simplification, not addition. Any new creation is just that, a creation; and it will be surely based on a perception or belief you carry as ego at that time.

Who needs another mis-perception to deal with later?

We are becoming empty of all of this. We are allowing Joy, Peace of Mind, and Love to flow to us and through us, from the depth of us. What else do I really need?

A return to our default state as Pure Spirit.

Stay simple.

I would like to devote the rest of 301 to expanding this further, granulize it down, down, down, using our main tool given by Jeshua many years ago.

Love

allows all things

trusts all things

embraces all things

trans-forms all things

trans-cends all things

trans-mutes all things

Love is all things

By the way

say this often

say this to yourself

say it to others to try it on,

they will be surprised

and who knows you may meet a fellow traveller.

Love allows all things.

There is no intervention. Whatever comes up in the mind is allowed.

Just a little more. This does not mean you have to sit there and allow your body to be run over by a bus. (smile).

We are talking about allowing in the mind, not necessarily things to do with the body. Although sometimes they do overlap a little. Body is out of Mind.

So whatever comes up in the mind is always allowed.

It can float through the mind and out the other side,

with just a watch

with no action

maybe a smile

can be caught

can be held to be examined

or

you can let it completely over run you, for a drama exercise, a few tears or some other suffering

a slide or fly left experience

a fly right victory

or

can be for great Joy

or

can be something to sing about.

You choose.

If you feel yourself flying left, this is usually into fear with automatic reactions. You can sit for the ride if you want to and become the watcher.

Now that is a fun idea.

You will fly left for a little, maybe a few loops, but as you allow opening for the feelings, rather than shutting down around them, you will start banking right.

Go for the flight! You could crash and burn, but remember, you instantly continue life when you hit the ground, you bounce and it is not fatal when it is mind stuff.

It doesn't matter (smile)—those words again!

So allow any of these moments to come to you in greater detail, open to them, allow a fuller experience.

The very opposite of why they exist, which is to scare you and control you and shut you down.

So now you can see how powerful Love is. It allows you to experience fear differently. That idea by itself is such an amazing thing to know that it may be enough for some.

So Love allows all things

Any thought. It doesn't mean you have to act on it.

But let's go further with this simplicity.

Love trusts all things.

You might as well allow this to happen also. Start trusting that everything coming up now is directly for you to examine and work with. Start trusting the invisible as knowing more than your ego self in body.

It may seem very odd at first to trust the invisible, especially if you consider yourself to be rational or intellectual.

However, you have got yourself into a mess, and what makes you think you can get yourself out of the mess, your way?

A mind full of dreams, illusions, delusions, an insane mind, an ego mind, almost always flies left and has done so for humanity for millennia.

How are all the ego minds doing??

You will probably say 'yes yes, that is why I want to learn to fly right'.

Good answer. Desires.

So trust the invisible again. Listen to the small quiet voice from the invisible.

This loving voice may not always talk, but it will always bring up Loving thoughts, ideas, and answers for you.

So sit inside the fearful feelings and allow them to be there. Settle down into them. Do not run away and hide or change the subject or project them at someone else.

Settle down into it, go quiet for a change, sink into it, lie down with it, invite it to come closer. Open to trusting that this has been brought to you, for you to sit with, to examine and feel.

It has been sent to you, by you, to be with *now*.

Remember the meek will inherit the earth. Trusting fits this criterion.

And as you settle down and settle down, and settle down, deeper and deeper into the only mind that exists that is holy, wholesome, true—some call it Christ mind—allow and trust everything.

It doesn't really matter what names are given to the one mind. Make up your own word.

You will know you are inside something very grand as you sink, and settle, and allow and trust.

You will open, you can open to this, you are opening to this, you are now floating beside the feeling or even inside the feeling.

You can explore feeling.

Explore this feeling.

Explore it slowly; become curious about this.

Be thorough. Go over it as if it is a new lover.

What is this thing??

You will find as you breathe and float with it, you will be able to look at this and see, yes, and say yes, know, yes, trust now and allow this amazing thought to come very clearly to you.

I am the owner of this or any of these feelings.

I actually created this curious thing that I am so afraid of.

and

I was going to fly left because of it!

Hmmm, amazing, where does all this come from?

Who wrote the script for this game?!

So now as you simplify and drop the fear and move to a more comfortable mental spot, you can ask to see the whens, hows, whats, and even maybe whys of this creation, and it will be given to you.

Given as thoughts, ideas, voice, your and other voices, movies (usually super vision), music, exact smell, touch, taste, clear remembrance of the events, the other people, times, many times. A string of times from its creation to the present.

And these words above are of course

Love Allowing and Trusting, and also now

Love embracing all these things.

So instead of sitting down with a movie or a book or the tablet or going to the gym, or having a beer, etc., to divert your mind: sit down, maybe lie down, settle down, sink down, and allow, trust, embrace those very important moments that arise for you.

You can even say to friends, 'Tonight I am not coming out. I am going on a mental discovery to a most wonderful place.'

And if it doesn't seem suitable at that moment to sink down, for instance if you are driving a car, know this: you can recreate this any time.

From my experience, I have found the best time is about 1:00 to 4:00 a.m. All the ego minds are sleeping around you. So little interference in the communication channels. At this time of night, you can drift up almost to awakening, and you can float in a most beautiful mind space and remake the situations and experiences with healing, and sometimes even have an unseen audience cheer you on. Yes.

So we are now getting deeper into the mechanics of creation.

This information applies to all created things.

(I will let you mull on that idea.)

A creator can see their creations; they can identify with them and know at some point they desired this to happen.

Even if it was as a two- or three-year-old child, seemingly wildly creating cause from some fearful event or experience, with effects that stay around for a lifetime.

A creator knows they keep their creations alive by feeding mind energy to them. Attention, it is called. Whatever you value, there your attention will be.

A creator knows that their creations are unreal and don't really exist, other than through pseudo methods, contrivances, as dreams, non-realities, virtual play on the movie screen of your mind, illusions, etc.

Some seem very real, but they are only floating

there because of you, as the master of that creation. You are the projector and the screen.

A creator also knows they can straighten out a creation like a panel beater or body worker and make it all Joyful again. Just slide out the scary parts and slide in some Loving parts.

A creator knows they can withdraw energy at any moment and end the creation.

And so with that, we now enter into the concept of Karma, which will be the basis of much of the discussion from now on. We have been discussing Karma, but we have not named it that yet.

(Cause and Effect) = Karma

A Creator exists outside ego karma.

They actually create their cause and effects at will, inside mind as virtualities, and at any moment can turn it all off and walk away whistling and smiling. No stickiness!

Karma runs inside ego mind and seemingly inside creations when you hold the cause and effect in place with seriousness.

It is running in your life as you slide or fly left. Karma is very simple to understand; it is no mystery.

Karma is just experiencing effect, driven by a cause laid down in the mind at some point, and then you lose contact with the fact that you made cause, and it can be scary when the effects arise or re-act for you.

You could call it a wild feral creation that you seem to have lost contact with.

That is all that needs to be said about Karma at present.

Ego Karma is Un-real. It has no Reality.

We will, however, use the idea or concept of Karma again and again as we progress through the chapters.

Did you get that?

Tell your friends that!

And now we move to a thought of amazement.

Simplicity leads to great Power—the exact opposite of the ego.

As Love flows, as simplicity envelops your mind and you become empty of all things that are fearful, guilty, and judgmental, you conversely become full of all things Loving—your cup overflows.

So empty-headedness and not knowingness (that

is, a healed mind) leads to great power, to great Love, to a new Viewpoint and a true perception, a new world of possibilities.

Maybe with new creations that are good, holy, and beautiful.

Maybe a thought has arisen in your mind of being a co-creator of Heaven on Earth!

Well guess what—you are already being this.

Those are Jeshua's words and ideas, but they are universal and timeless, in fact outside time.

And in closing…

I would like to wrap up the whole discussion in two new concepts for you, already mentioned but now more personally fitted.

You can wrap yourselves up in these also; in fact, I think they may be your favourite clothes now, that is, spiritual clothes.

Self Love and Forgiveness.

If you have got to this word, you are starting to wrap yourself in Self Love. You must Love yourself greatly now. You can have a few tears of Joy about that, and it is OK.

Yes, allow this, trust this, and embrace this as feeding for your soul.

Your inner child (not the human child but the cosmic child) will also be so pleased to know that Love is being allowed now. Fear can dissipate.

Wrap yourself in your Self Love.

You may have been told that this is selfish and unseemly. Another mis-perception based on culture or religion.

Self Love always translates into Love and compassion for other as you have found out so many times.

Now all the allowing, the trusting, the embracing is your Self Love. Your desire to awaken, to heal, to be enlightened, to become light, to fly right, has led you to find that it was you yourself that you have been looking for all this time. All answers are inside you, all Love is inside you, closer than your breath and less than the width of a thought away, always and forever.

You are intimately bound to the whole cosmos, with no separation.

And Forgiveness.

More Self Love will spin from this, each time you Forgive yourself of a mis-perception.

It is very clear now, no one has ever done anything to you.

You do not have to forgive anyone. They have done nothing to you. You have made it all up, and hence each time you are aware that you have just healed, or dropped some energy about a fearful creation that you created, you can say:

> *I forgive myself for ever thinking this was true or real; it was only a dream, an illusion, an unreal moment, an insanity, >>>>>> it is my creation.*

So forgive yourself often as you bathe in the experiences of flying right.

Actually it may not matter if you fly left or right; if you are a master pilot, you will always end up flying right anyway.

Sort of like Psalm 23.

Pat yourself on the back and acknowledge yourself with Self Love and Self-Forgiveness.

There is much more to say below this level, but I feel it suffices with this at this time.

And now you enter into experience rather than words.

See, it is only experience.

Words are symbols of symbols, twice removed from reality. (ACIM)

Words try to convey ideas and thoughts, and these we know now are not reality.

Ideas and thoughts are one step away and are also not real.

Only experience can allow you to be in reality as your True Self.

So in closing again:

Go quietly and marvel at the moments arriving for you.

Watch the mystery of life surrounding you as you allow, trust, and embrace, and fall into the True Mind once again.

Until I return again in the next chapter.

(This next line was in the original letters.)

I do not know what it will be, but I will allow, trust and embrace as it arises from the grand one mind and the mystery behind it.

How's the Viewpoint??
Well done.
Love to you all

Shamaré—The Guardian, the Protector, the Door Keeper, and the Gate Keeper

Addendum

Ownership of Creations

In Spirituality 301, we were left with the discussion on the various facets of being a creator.

And so, we all now know we are fundamentally creators, in imitation of the grand sustaining mystery of Reality that birthed us and flows from the depth of us.

So how has it been for you, as you watch and take ownership of your creations?

Up until this point in our various discussions, it may have actually seemed that you only need to fly right when you get re-active about something or feel poorly or slide emotionally in present time.

Well, this is always a good place to start, as these situations are very immediate and noticeable. By now, though, I am almost sure you will be questioning other things in your life.

So to start our process together this time, I want you to stop right now whatever you are doing, just stop, and look at your surroundings and then reflect on your life and see that all your thoughts that have become creations have led you to this very moment.

What are your surroundings like? What are your friends like? What state are you living in? If you have a partner, do you treat them lovingly? How are you with your family members? If you have children, are you encouraging them with unconditional love and praise to become clear grand creators also? How is the body's health? Do you have a strong belief structure? Do you believe you are right about your belief structure? Are you anxious, nervous, frightened by events, are you controlled by superstitions—intellectual, religious, old age or new age? Are you controlled by another's thoughts, books, words, or even presence?

The list is huge. It is every facet of life you have and are creating, directly or indirectly.

All these creations are imbued with your allowing, trusting, and embracing. You hold them in place, alive, by bringing your attention to them, by placing value on them. Feeding them your mental attention or energy.

The list of questions above and many more are indicators of your creations.

And if you say you don't like your creations or some

of them, you are merely in judgment of your own creations.

Not a big deal, as you will see.

Take a moment, regularly.

Just Stop and Review.

If you are finding you are not in Joy and a Peaceful state, and Love doesn't seem to be in the equation, some questions can be asked.

Say, for example, that you have a strong belief pattern about food (or anything else).

Yes, the long list of dos and don'ts, shoulds and shouldn'ts. Some food may be dangerous or OK. A long list of dualities held in place by so-called knowledge.

Consider this and ask yourself:

Is this a belief that serves me well? Does it bring Peace and Joy to me, or am I always in fear of certain aspects of food?

It may be time to simplify or return to Joy about food, with thanksgiving.

These questions can cover all aspects of your beliefs or intellectual pursuits or culture or life patterns or religion, even family energy or just old habits and viewpoints.

As we know by now, simplicity always leads to Joy and Peace as you empty yourself of the need to be right about all these things.

Who really cares? Well, of course, someone who wants to be right!

So here is some additional info to help you create and allow Peace and Joy to flow into your life as human.

We have now arrived at a point where you can re-work what seems like difficult old creations or old scary events. This discussion brings focus to them, and you will see they are not a big deal after all.

When I first spoke to Jeshua many years ago, I felt at the time that somehow the meeting was not overly warm and friendly, and it didn't seem satisfactory to me.

I asked him about these feelings in a later discussion, and he said this:

'How would you like it to be? Go back and change it to the way you want it to be!'

At the time, I didn't quite understand this, and it

seemed an odd thing to do, *as I was sure I was right about the situation.* (**Smile about that one**.)

It wasn't until sometime later that I started to realise the key to the seeming dilemma.

Any event you have not liked or lost your Joy and Peace inside of can be changed by simply addressing what really was transpiring at that moment. It takes awareness and again watching and catching your mind at work.

For some reason, I lost Joy and Peace at that moment with Jeshua. Something about it disturbed my Peace, and of course it had to be one of my creations I had made for myself beforehand.

All I needed to do to fix the meeting was to revisit that older creation I had made that caused the loss of Joy and Peace, then rework it or release it, and the meeting and talk with Jeshua would change also, following the mental release of beliefs and expectations that caused the feelings in the first place.

This creation that was Cause, of course, was not made while I was talking with him, but earlier. At that moment with Jeshua, I was in Effect and I needed to go to past original Cause.

There was a belief or a mis-understanding or mis-perception in me, a cultural habit maybe, that said that events have to be this way or that way for them to be acceptable or correct or right.

That realisation of this mis-perception in itself is sometimes enough to heal a past event.

Therefore, you can heal your mind if you forgive yourself for thinking you know how the mechanism of Joy and Peace should always work for you.

See that! My so-called ego knowing in action had led me to flying left. I was expecting a certain way and outcome and it didn't come, so I made a slide happen or a fly left. I bounced off an old Cause and had the Effect right while I was talking to him.

When Love is flowing to you, and you receive it, allow it, trust and embrace it, you know then that this is the only way for Joy and Peace to flow in your mind. Not your proscribed way that has to fit your beliefs.

So in that moment with Jeshua, Love was not flowing in me. I had some belief of how it should be before I would be happy.

My so-called ego knowledge had to do with a belief on how relationships and communication should be before Love could flow to me, and only then would I feel Joy and Peace.

What I called happiness was a construct, a fabrication on my terms only. It was made up, a creation that I thought was better than true Joy and Peace.

I was making conditions that had to be met before I could be happy and have joy and peace; and of course this type of joy and peace was ego-made and devoid of reality. The joy was fleeting rather than continuously flowing.

Amazing ego arrogance or ignorance or both.

Do you get all of this??

I was creating a scenario in which I had expectations of how it should be before the event even happened. It, the belief, was sitting there waiting to jump out and do its thing. I had already sabotaged the outcome before the meeting.

I had to have things a certain way before I would feel all right. It had to be my way, and my way led to loss of Joy and Peace.

Looking at it now, I am sure Jeshua knew this already and acted as a mirror for me.

No wonder I had many other difficulties also. What a revelation that was!

So all I had to do was re-visit the earlier creation I had made of how it should be and release the needs and expectations I had. This Cause was not required any longer, as it stopped Love flowing to me from the depth of me, in certain conditions.

Then that moment with Jeshua is healed, and **my now feeling** of it would change magically, with Love flowing, in a state of Peace and Joy, as I listened to him chat to me.

Do you understand this? Did you get it??

So any conversation, any event, any drama can be changed, just as it said in 301, by you becoming a panel beater or body worker and straightening out the bumps and wrinkles. Just by sliding in the new parts, and you have a new event. Healing the so-called past, actually present.

And of course, this newly allowed event now has Joy Peace and Love flowing in it naturally, without any effort on your or my behalf.

The return to Reality and the natural.

In Spirituality 501 we are going to address a much broader discussion on this. This broader discussion brings even greater Joy and Peace. I have been given a glimpse of this discussion already.

And of course, as you broaden out on this, you become light itself, or enlightenment, bringing light in a world of darkness—a world that is trapped, it seems, in the very narrow focus of Ego mind. A very small and myopic existence, as a self-identified group of humans with huge limits.

So here is a very good test for you as creator or body worker:

The making of new pieces for the vehicle of experience.

Take an event, preferably one with some heat in it, as it is a larger body of energy and will act as a good prototype for you to practise on. Something you can get your teeth into and hammer out the wrinkles.

Some event that causes fear to rise up as you remember it again. (Remembering is just putting some new members or legs on it and letting it loose like a wild horse again.)

Oh my god, not that memory! Yes, *that* one. Pick it up out of the bag and let it loose, and then—just as you do with the normal flying right technique—start to allow, trust, and embrace this event.

Yahoo, ride 'em cowboy! (Or cowgirl or cowperson or cowhuman.)

See, it is no different. There is no time outside ego or world. There are only events.

So now hone in on the creation that you made; find what is Cause or causing all the bucking and snorting.

See that you own this creation; you actually created it. Then move to seeing that if you drop this creation, you will move to a larger mind space, more freedom, more laughter.

So practise this flying right technique on every and any event, now or then.

Who really cares when it happened? Maybe ten lifetimes ago or last week or a minute ago. The game is freedom from fear.

Now a little encouragement for you all.

You know by now that this is a true path; nothing else can or will work permanently.

Only you can heal yourself. There are no saviours that will do it for you.

Saviours encourage, are full of compassion, and only see Love in you. They never see your ego as real.

So please be very gentle on yourselves. You have now found gold; it is your treasure.

Take your time. En-Joy this work. It is holy work, or a bit of a hoot, depending on your viewpoint.

Some of you may be able to float up a balloon of experience, jump in, go for a ride and let all the gas out, and come back down very quickly.

Others may have difficulty even launching.

Remember the keys.

Desire, Intention, Allowance, and Surrender.

Then run the mantra on Love.

Keep your desire strong, and place intention right on in your enlightenment project and then slowly drop resistance and allow, allow, allow and slide into embrace as Love is flowing again.

Surrender into the divine that is only inside you, nowhere else. You are divine and loved beyond measure. That is why when you open your petals to the light, love flows from the depth of you, to you (your awareness) and through you, and you can give as much to others as you wish. It is an endless supply.

By the way, embracing a fear by gritting your teeth and forcing it always fails.

There is no healing inside ego.

If you say 'I can't feel this', it really means you have a resistance that needs dropping. Dropping resistance comes by taking value out of the fear.

Resistance is borne of seriousness, and the best thing for seriousness is light or light-heartedness, or silliness. As Jeshua has said to one serious one, 'Tell yourself a joke or two each day'.

So seriousness is a fly left. Stop, catch it, bag it. Say 'I caught myself getting serious again', and laugh or chuckle until it dissolves.

If you really want to get serious about getting un-serious, then start to push your boundaries out. Join a public speaking group, a drama class, a singing class, a dance class. Get out there and break loose. Even try being a stand-up comic by telling jokes, even if you fluff up. This will invoke all sorts of re-activity, and you can deal with that and expand, expand, laughing and crying all the while.

And finally, to wrap up this chapter, a little to ponder on. Sort of like a little homework for you.

(Jeshua taught us this one also.)

You may like to try this out. You can provoke yourself in order to find hidden creations. Things you are unaware of about yourself.

Say to yourself, 'I am loved, I am loving, I am loveable'.

Then again, with feeling, open up this time, breathe and be still as you say the words in your mind or out loud.

Another good way is to sit with a friend and say this one after another, looking openly in the eye of the other person as you say it.

They will know whether you are in feeling or just being a robot or forcing it.

Keep saying this until you get to a differentiation on the feelings on each phrase.

Which one has the most resistance on it? That is the one to ponder more deeply.

What is it about me that feels that way about that phrase, or those words? Muss on it.

Say the three statements several times a day, and

a picture will form about this. When it is very clear, start flying right as you say the words, open to the one with resistance.

You might feel, yes, I am loved, yes, I am loving, but there is no way I am loveable.

Well, look carefully at your life. You will be experiencing this.

Or any one of the other two.

Good pondering and flying till next chapter.

In the original notes this was the last chapter before Xmas or Christ Mass, as it were.

You may like to have a different Christmas this year.

Christmas is not only about Jesus or Jeshua, it is fundamentally about you.

You will by now have touched the Christ mind many times as you worked on your creations. This is where you dwell perpetually; it is actually your home.

So celebrate the re-birth of yourself this Christmas. Toast yourself as having had a most wonderful year in discovering your True Self again.

You are the Return of the Christ, that is the bringing of Christ Mind to earth again.

You are the one who is bringing heaven to earth. All that old religious stuff is a mis-understanding.

The focus has been on the one who was the prototype for us, the mirror, the metaphor, and everyone has missed the point for some 2000 years.

This mis-understanding is now ending and will float away as an old creation or belief, worn out, to be re-placed with a rising tide of humanity who understand it is really about them.

Many are embracing this new idea now. Embrace yourself this Xmas. And if you have family, embrace them with that understanding, because it changes everything.

So Merry Christmas to you all.

May Love flow to you grandly from the divine depths of you, and Joy and Peace be your companion always.

Does that sound sort of Xmas-like?

Let that Love that flows to you, from the depth of you, flow through you and out to others. As you allow this, more flows to you and a grand exponential flow starts.

The receiving and the giving.

I receive free, I give free. I receive freely, I give freely.

'Here, have some, it is good for you.'

How's the Viewpoint??
Well done.
Love to you all

Shamaré—The Guardian, the Protector, the Door Keeper, and the Gate Keeper

Spirituality 401

You Are Light

The last chapter, 301 Addendum, was a continuation on the theme of being a creator who has power to make and break their creations, to modify and improve and also delete.

That is how powerful you are, and you have been doing this since the beginning.

And this beginning is in need of discussion, also.

Spirituality 501 will lead us back to the beginning of all things.

In this communication, Spirituality 401, we need to discuss light. There is so much said about light.

Our pathway is to enlightenment, or the recovery of the light we seem to have lost. It is only an illusion of loss. We moved our attention from Reality full of light to a created domain, and we got caught in a dream of mis-identification with many seeming shadows and with darkness.

So to begin our discussion on light, we have some

written records about it that seem to have survived time and come with a very meaningful message for us all.

Jeshua ben Joseph—as the first human, it seems, to have fully cleared out of their mind the illusional dream of losing the light, then recovered and held the Christed minded state—said quite a few interesting things back 2000 years ago.

At the so-called famous Sermon on the Mount, he addressed a group who turned up to hear him speak. There is no record of who was present, but we have been told now that it was a large crowd with a high percentage of females, but suffice to say it could have been Jews of different sects, Romans, Greeks, Samaritans, or any of the people present in Palestine at that moment.

It doesn't say what type of people they were, or allude to morality, culture, ethics, beliefs, or viewpoints.

There is one thing we can be sure of, and that is they were all in ego mind—so, basically like people today.

The address carried this startling statement:

'You are the light of the world'.

This was directed at everyone present without

exception. All and anybody at that meeting was regarded as the light of the world.

It was inclusive and not exclusive, so pure spirituality.

NB: Ego is into exclusive in a big way.

If you had been there, you would have been included (and you may have been).

So it is a universal attribute he spoke, and timeless. Spirituality is outside time.

Jeshua, in his eyes, had no failures in his listening group, no baddies, no losers, no not-good-enoughs, no sinners, etc. All inclusive, they were the light of this world. Amazing.

Before we discuss what this means, we must also include that Jeshua also said publicly at another time and place, 'I am the light of the world'.

So this statement shows first the equality of the first group at the Sermon on the Mount and Jeshua himself. And as it is inclusive, that includes you also right now.

There is nothing special about Jeshua other than that he is a very good mirror and model, friend and teacher for us.

If we now jump ahead 2000 years, forward to the 1990s, his greetings in our times have been:

'Greetings to the Children of Light Divine.'

At another time in the 90s, he said, 'You are brighter than 10,000 stars'.

And of course there are many other light references.

It is not unknown in most cultures about light. In fact, Divali, the Hindu Festival of Lights, is celebrated almost worldwide.

Many realise at some level they need to gain light, or light needs to be celebrated, as it is thought that light is a destroyer of darkness, which is a metaphor for divine over ego. The old play on dualities.

However, in Truth and Reality, we abide continually in light and have never left that.

We are exactly that, light itself, brighter than 10,000 stars.

Another very common discussion these days is about moving self to the light on body death. Many NDEs (near death experiences) report the light at the end of the tunnel.

By the way, the light at the end of the tunnel is your light that you are seeing.

There are even movies that make light of this tunnel of light idea. Sid the Sloth said to Diego the Sabre Tooth Tiger when he was dying, I think, 'Don't move to the light, old buddy', as a way to say, 'don't leave us bodily' or 'come back to body'.

So why bring this into play at this time?

I have sensed that some are having a great deal of self-generated difficulties or stickiness about not being able to separate identity of True Self from body self. (Notice the upper and lower cases.)

In 'A Course in Miracles', Jeshua says this is one of the sticky spots in awakening to our True Self, and that is dropping body identification.

So Light is a very good metaphor for True Self and its State.

And of course, many cultures regard God as Light or the Bringer of Light. And again this shows the very tight linkage to the divine mystery that birthed us and ourselves, as we reside inside the Mystery Reality itself as a part.

We are made in that mystery's image, and it must be Light, bathed and supported in the energy of Love.

And so with that preamble about Light and the Divine, we arrive at another point that needs to be said. We are god or divine itself, as there is no separation, as has been said many times so far. We are closer to the divine mystery than our body breath, even closer than the width of one of our thoughts.

We are like amalgam, fused together inseparably to the divine.

The same substance.

That is why we can say without contradiction,

This is

How safe you are

How loved you are

How everything really you are.

This is actually all that does truly exist. There is nothing else. Only the one thing turning, and we are that one thing.

So contemplate that. Ponder that one.

Ego may jump a little, but smile and move through it and drop stickiness. Surrender to this concept and it will lead you to the Reality of it.

So inside this time and 3D space domain, it is god divine experiencing god divine across the perceptional divide, even in dream.

So play well and have fun; you would not want to disappoint the other side would you?? (That is a joke of course, smile.)

And hence again 2000 years ago, Jeshua was called Emmanuel—'God is with us'. True for you, too, when identification is switched back to Spirit.

Maybe those ancient people were keyed in a little more tightly than we suspected.

God divine participating inside an egoic creation, now there is a game to play.

And you are doing well.

And it can be

oh so serious as human

or

oh so much fun as human.

Original notes:

'Now it has also come to my attention that many

are playing the flying right game and are en-Joying it, which is super. Some with outstanding happenings.'

I would like to encourage everyone to jump in and play and feel the power that comes with this.

Some are saying to me something like this:

I fly right and say, 'I don't need to go left any more, I do not need or want that old behaviour now'.

Careful, this has a small tinge of ego running through it.

Maybe the thought is something like this:

I don't like this reaction, and I don't really want this anymore. Fear or guilt a judgment against self.

Maybe this is an attempt to throw it away from you.

Just to make sure you trans-form, remember, and you do remember, that in ego there is no healing. There is only more of the same, the insanity.

Only Love flowing from the depth of your divine Self can heal. Not faith, not hope, not good deeds, not praying to some saviour, not pleading for help, not trying to throw it away, will ever work.

Only a return to the remembrance of who you

really are and the surrender to Love's flow will bring healing.

Some say, 'I believe in God, I have faith, I have hope that he or she can fix me'.

God doesn't see the problem in you, as you are only in a dream and it is not real. He or she is too busy loving you. Jeshua again.

Only you can start this healing, by opening the windows and doors to your mind and heart, to Love flowing to and through you, from the depth of you, god divine deep. Surrender.

God divine flowing through you as God divine.

May I add...

Rather than rush through these arising moments, stop, breathe, slow down; the moment has arrived for you. Allow it, trust it, go deeper, go much deeper, go deep deep. Breathe into the feeling of re-activity and feel the tight connection with creator Self.

You are that creator.

Feel it, feel it. Don't leave it too quickly. Feel it. Move into it. Do not throw it away casually. Feel it, embrace it, hold it.

It is your gift to yourself.

Stay with it, feeling and playing with it for a while and en-Joy the release by Love itself.

the allowing

the trusting

the embracing

the trans-forming

the trans-cending

the trans-mutating

the alchemy

You will then know the power that is yours. And all power has been given you. Naturally.

You can drop fear; everything is now available for you to heal.

You will start to notice at some point and may say to yourself at times:

'I am not the same now. It is quieter, it is easier, it is Peaceful, I am changed, and I am en-Joying this life more now. I am not in such a hurry to move through things. I like to watch and muse and feel it all.'

And this expansion is certain.

When you re-act and tighten up with stress, you drive light out of your body—literally, the cells contract, the DNA shortens.

When Love is flowing through you, your cells relax and expand and your DNA lengthens and lights up.

Check this. Also ask a scientist who knows.

You may actually be re-encoding your DNA in your body to a new resonance, a forgotten ancient song, that is now arising again in you.

You often say this about another.

'They were so full of light, they were literally glowing.'

Have you noticed that laughter does this—it seems to pump the body with light.

It is the mental attitude of laughter, **care free—fear free**.

So the game now of course is:

Fly right and get all puffed up, or should that be fluffed up with light??

I want you to move past mediocrity or just trying to do this, but move to becoming Master of Self.

And of course as you master, you will also teach.

Another something to ponder about for you:

As you enter simplification, you will notice it smooths out, the bumps are less, the road is clearer.

And as you do not know from moment to moment what is next, you actually may not be living life itself anymore, but life is living you now.

How is this possible, you becoming master and this allowing life to live you? If you are living as one, you are all things, and the will of the one thing is what is really happening. This is the whole life, the true life, the Real life.

So you might as well get the ego out of the way and allow that life to live you. Why paddle upstream anymore!

By the way, this is probably a very good place to fix up some other things that seem to be in the way or in the air.

There are so many books and people speaking now about so-called spiritual things, and the word ego is bandied about easily, and it seems like many would have you believe that this is the enemy that must be conquered.

Our reference on any matter is always these simple words you can use to test out some of these or any other statements or ideas:

What is Real cannot be threatened

What is un-real doesn't exist

Herein lies the Peace of god.

ACIM

Where does the ego reside?

In the un-real camp, it does not exist in Reality. Self-created. Tick.

And yet many would have you fight this monster and talk endlessly about it and miss, 'That only Love is Real'. Tick.

To give some level of substance to this, let's look at Jeshua's story on the importance of the ego. A summary of it, of course:

Once in a mountain valley, in the remotest distance of a land that no one ever goes to or walks in, on a mountain slope, an alpine flower spreads out its tiny petals and casts a shadow on the ground, so small. No one noticed, no one knew, no one remembers.

This is the ego.

It has no importance, no power, no effect. It is not noticed in the universe.

It casts a very, very small shadow.

Claim your place by being diligent and disciplined in your mind and laugh at this small un-real shadow.

The four keys again for you are:

Desire, Intention, Allowance, and Surrender.

If you are still reading, tick desire.

Intention is yours to do as you will, but essential.

Intention and Allowance are the flying-right fluffy-light game.

Surrender is Spirituality 501 to 601 to come.

In 301, I left you with a little pondering to do.

So how did you get on with the Loving, Loved, Loveable?

It is a good way to play the flying right game by yourself.

Did you get a differentiation feeling off the words?

Have you got to the bottom of this?? It is sometimes a very deep hole.

Do not be in a great hurry to burst these things. En-Joy them.

As Jeshua has said several times, en-Joy the hell out of them.

Much revelation will come from these ponderings. Note them and be aware you have stored all these up to guide you back to light itself, at the right time, your time.

Dedicate some time each day now to Self. In fact, several times each day.

Nothing is hidden from you.

All is available for you.

You are Light itself.

Last point, my dear friends: What has been shared is very advanced, and you know it all.

To reach that point may seem a way away. >>> Choose.

The day will come

and

The dream and illusion will clear and Reality will reappear.

How's the Viewpoint??
Well done.
Love to you all

Shamaré—The Guardian, the Protector, the Door Keeper, and the Gate Keeper

Addendum

I am the one I have been searching for

Spirituality 401 may still be sitting in your mind. It was a big step with much to contemplate.

However, it makes perfect sense, and a mind that is open will dissolve into this new state without too much of a fight.

And so now we can talk more openly and freely and without hesitation about what might strike the ego mind, as you now know how safe you really are at all moments.

Nothing can interfere with you, except you.

As awareness expands, it leads to many new and very exciting opportunities. A new corrected perception opens, and a new discussion starts all over again.

'I am new, I am free, I am loved, loving, and loveable, I am linked to all things, I am all things, I am nourished by the one thing that truly exists, I am that I am.'

This is the grand Reality state of being, being new, being free, being loved, being linked, etc.

I am that—I am.

I am not what I thought I was. It was a mis-perception, a mis-understanding, an error on my part. A Viewpoint that gave experiences of illusion and dreams and separateness with guilt and fear, with endless judgments.

I turned my attention away into fear, guilt, and judgment long ago, and now I return my attention to Reality. A new Viewpoint has opened for me.

As I look up the stream to Love flowing to me as Spirit, flowing from the divine, and I look down the stream and see my trans-mutation of Love to states of fear and guilt still flowing out of me as an illusional human.

However, I can now, after many eons, see through the mist again and see and be aware of Love flowing to me. I can feel this flow to me and through me and in me from the depth of me, from the divine, not from a source outside of me. I exist because of this.

And to think that all of this time I have been looking outside myself for answers to the dilemma!

In books maybe, a god separate from you, a saviour, gurus maybe or family advice or teachers or experts.

'It was me that I was looking for all this time.'

I am the most direct portal to the Love that flows to me. I can explore this.

I open myself to this portal and say, 'Flood me in Love and Light'.

As an amalgam of the one thing, as a part of the one thing, of same substance, same nature, I now open myself to this nature, this vibration, this seemingly new song, truly an old resonance.

No longer do I resonate with the illusion and insanity of the tiny shadow called the ego that doesn't exist in this only Reality.

I am free at last, as I awaken from the dream of the dreamer.

And I need more of this. I need more of this nature, this resonance, more and more; fill me with this new elixir. (Jeshua 2000 years later still expanding.)

The mystery of mysteries is my source of all things. My origin.

Who is this one? It is me, linked to eternity and to infinity.

That is how deep my mystery goes! How to know the mystery??

There is only one feed in the universe. It is pure and true.

It is all-inclusive and has no judgment, no cost, all Loving.

That feed runs in you, through you, from the deepest depth of you, and you have this amazing freedom to do as you will with it.

You have awareness and consciousness granted to you for eternity, from the mystery of all things.

Your individuation is certain forever. How you allow Love to feed this is your affair. But in Reality, it is a choiceless choice.

Note: Nothing can be done in this 3D space and time domain to avail yourself of this feed of Love and Light.

It all happens on the other side, in Reality where you are always present.

Hence Spirituality is the focus now.

The place where this all happens is in mind, the one universal spot where all individuation rests in experience.

The gift of this experience is something that can now be appreciated with greater and greater excitement, as all things now make sense again.

I would have more of this, you say.

Fly right, fly into fear and guilt and judgment and feel all that you have created.

It will dissolve.

The mist will dissolve.

There is no other way, no wishing and hoping.

It is individuated responsibility—take it.

You are OK, you always have been.

All you did was trans-mute Love into another form, using alchemy, a sleight of hand, for experiences. From gold to lead, rather than the other way around.

And now you know that you can trans-mute to higher states, to greater purity. (It seems.)

Why not! Only you will know the answer, if you are honest about it all.

And about everything else?

Yes, yes, the big bang was the realisation by us

all that light could become matter through a combined, agreed, group thought, a transmutation, a multi-handed grand manifestation.

An evolution of mind, a giant step into the experience of:

'What would it be like to live in a world without only Love.'

Next—Heaven on Earth awaits.

How's the Viewpoint??
Well done.
Love to you all

Shamaré—The Guardian, the Protector, the Door Keeper, and the Gate Keeper

Spirituality 501

Heaven On Earth Awaits

If you have reached this chapter, you are progressing along this pathway.

However, some are saying, 'I am still struggling'.

En-Joy it. It is just part of the unfolding.

You must convince yourself that you can recover yourself, not me or any other source convincing you.

Find your own way through this.

In the illusional 3D space and time experience, it may seem appropriate to struggle right now.

In Reality it is not necessary. It is only a choice away.

I forgive myself for believing in struggle. >> Say it if necessary

Amen (or So be it, or I now accept this as the real truth for me) and live from that.

Just a little encouragement to keep moving.

It may seem like dis-location, difficult or even painful at times, continue through. You have asked for this change.

We will discuss this pain in depth later.

And now to 501, a graduation to seemingly higher states of being.

You will recall the long encouragement, and by now you must be approaching semi-expert status in flying right into fear, guilt, and judgment, and using the steps of allowing Love to flow into this surrender. The steps—allowing, trusting, embracing, trans-forming, trans-cending, trans-muting, and being healed out the other side as Love itself.

When this process is repeated long enough, the mind will start to clear of mis-perceptions, and a new viewpoint—the New Viewpoint, an awareness opening—will start to show itself.

This type of question will arise at some point, or at several points along the way, even early on:

How many times do I have to do this?

It seems like there is an ocean of trans-forming required. I am full of rubbish?!

Smile on that question and judgment as it arises. It will arise quite frequently. Also this one:

Will I ever trans-cend all of this??

And gradually, with patience and application, a new awareness will develop, a new possibility starts to emerge and show itself to you.

If I can be and hold just this one thing, illusion will end very quickly.

How is this possible?

We can go back to our very cryptic discussion on Karma, seemingly long ago now, and use this as the stepping stones to understanding.

Karma is just Cause and Effect.

In healing, you use Effect as the window or doorway or gateway to access Cause.

Shamaré: Ancient Hebrew >> guardian, protector, gate keeper and door keeper

A Summary.

The flying right into fear, guilt, and judgment is to fly directly into Effect, the emotion, the re-activity that arises at that moment.

So you fly into Effect (door, gate, window, maybe

stargate!) and breathe and fall, breathe and fall, increase awareness, gain Peace of Mind with embrace and through this Effect's gate or window or door, finally walk and arrive at original Cause.

There is *always* a tunnel leading Effect back to Cause. Breathe down it. Sometimes there are doors along the way that are locked; find the key and keep moving to Cause.

Cause is the original creation laid down, which the Effect spins off every time.

In the moment of Effect, the only method of healing is to fly right and land in Cause, in a Peaceful embraced state.

This is how all healing comes: a Peaceful state is allowing Love to flow into Cause. There is no other way.

The world of illusional, intellectual thinking has told other ways. You can take a pill, do this -ism or -ology, this modality, just one more session or whatever—but if you do not flow Love into Cause, nothing changes. You remain unhealed, unaffected, and remain as the same or original creation with Cause and also Effect spinning.

Self Love is the beginning for this freedom.

Note—you may be lucky and find a therapist that

helps Love flow to you and through you as you progress down the road to freedom. Thank them.

This level of Therapist is usually aware that illusions are all you are seeing. They do not work with illusions, but rather they get you to move to Self Love as the beginning point. After that, it is all you.

Only reverse engineering Karma can lead to healing. And how is this possible for you? You made it All, so you know it All.

It is not a mystery to you, it is not hidden from you, it is not locked up in a vault without a key, it is not an ocean away or at the top of a mountain with an old guru sitting there. You are the old guru.

I labour the thought for you, as the next step is monumental for you and will be an 'aha' or 'thank heavens for that' or 'my god, amazing!' or even tears of Joy.

You have been practising flying right, and if you haven't and you aren't doing this several times a day by now, you may wish to consider going back to the beginning to restart.

What is about to be revealed can only come true for you if you are practised and disciplined in mind. It is Surrender.

The illusional or insane world is awash with cause

and with a multitudes of effects running through every moment, spinning from the individuated minds locked in ego—illusional, dreaming, insanity. Everyone is contributing. A grand creation of world, in all its diversity, madness, and so-called love. An illusion of huge proportions, of course, but in Reality it does not exist.

Very early, all the clues for this next grand step have been given, and it can be said to be a natural one, but oh my goodness, how far-reaching.

I am teasing you a little now because I want you on the edge of your chairs.

Only a few have managed this, but the floodgates are about to open in times ahead, as a crack first, then progressively more until it is a roaring torrent, and then silence.

You may recall that the world started with a single thought, leading to more thoughts, and each individuation is a matrix or tapestry of Thoughts, Identity, Personality, Karma, Cause and Effect.

Institutions are made to control this Karma—schools are made to imprint this, books are written to document it, cultures act as silent police forces (or not so silent sometimes) to hold it in place. Governments pass laws about it, religions link it to a vengeful god.

And yet our main pre-occupation is to break free and celebrate. Celebrate life with one another and bask in our light with one another and laugh and sing and be silly, find someone that will be our lover, to experience a Peaceful Mind and have Joyous times.

So the next step is so obvious and so simple.

The jostling of life, the great movement washing through all, hides the doorway, the gap of escape to freedom.

People walk past this every day and it is never seen, it is lost to their view, masked by victimhood, mis-perception, and mis-understanding.

The gap is small in the world. If everyone found it, the world would empty very quickly and heaven on earth would appear rapidly. It will at some point.

However, it will be progressive.

The doorway or gap is the eye of the needle.

It requires true aim to go through the eye, even a little spitting on the thread to make sure it doesn't catch as you thread it through.

How do you find and reach the eye of the needle?

Jeshua says he was sitting under a tree in Palestine

after his return from India when this thought came to him, and he held it close and en-acted it. The rest is his-story.

(Have you noticed many great things happen while sitting under trees? Maybe find a tree now and sit there and carry on reading.)

So without further ado, the process will be revealed to you.

You may not be able to avail yourself of this yet, but the day is definitely coming to rejoice about this.

So you start burrowing like a good rabbit. You find an effect—burrow, breathe, and fall—arrive at the cause, heal, find another effect, burrow, get the cause, heal. And if you keep going you would slowly discover that your very large rabbit warren was a pipe leading back and back and back, until one day you would come to the first effect ever; and pushing through this effect, there is first cause waiting for you.

This may take some time (lifetimes), as cause and effect have been running in this 3D space and time domain mindset for several billion years now.

That seems like a game-stopper.

Let's try something else.

You will recall the discussion on being able to change an event, effect, or cause anywhere in time.

In 'A Course in Miracles', Jeshua encourages us several times 'to look this day at first memories, first events, first effect, first cause'.

So when the day arrives and you have enough clarity and holiness, with a laugh and silliness running (yes, get out the gown, the crosses, the smoker, the holy water and candles):

'Maybe I can move my very clear attention and awareness to the first Cause and Effect and run (Surrender) the "allow, trust, embrace" routine across it, and puff—like rubbing Aladdin's lamp—I am in a magic world.'

If you unload first Cause and first Effect from your mind as a truth (or more correctly, as an illusional truth or a mis-understanding or a monumental mis-creation), it will literally be that, puff, eye of the needle and welcome home, collect your $200 and sit and have a glass of wine and relax and chat with family and friends at the homecoming party.

After that, this state is held with pure Surrender with untrans-muted Love flowing from the depth of you, from the divine.

And now we enter into the process inside time to bring this to fruition, as a fruit for you to pick.

Much of this is metaphorical as our language cannot express very well the situation at first Cause.

Embryonic Cosmic Child thinking, 'What would it be like to live in a world that is not just love?'

Yes, that is first Cause. It progressed.

First Effect spun off this as a reaction.

Guilt, Fear, and arising Judgment.

The Birth of Separation.

The mis-perception of seeing good and bad, the tree of knowledge of good and bad. The beginning of duality, rather than the one thing arising.

The beginning of all illusions and madness.

A world of thoughts spun from this, and you sitting there reading this are definitely part of the thoughts.

However, True You, not dreaming-in-illusion you, is fine, OK, not touched. Love is still flowing, sustaining all, it is OK.

I will leave this discussion here to let you ponder this grand step.

Muse on it until you read the Spirituality 501 Addendum, as this information is enough for this offering.

It is Monumental, a giant jump in awareness and possibilities.

To round it out a little, it is like the very tired traveller finally reaching the top of mountain path and squeezing through the last gap in the path, finding them self in a new world, Shangri-La.

The Ascended Masters, in body or spirit already present, the Awakened Ones, will surround the new arrival and welcome him back from his dream, the journey of no distance. Another one home.

What seemed like an eternity is only a blink, as it took no time either, as time is missing from Shangri-La, hence Eternal life.

Still remaining in body at this point means an instantly trans-formed Viewpoint, to heaven on earth for that one.

They will all say, 'An enlightened one walks amongst us again'.

Only Love arises in this one, no fear, guilt, or judgment, a new Christ mind is present.

All Cause and Effect is gone. Ego Karma healed.

The game begins anew.

New parameters, a new way of being, a new creation, with no thought of separation or loss or gain, only Joy, a Peaceful Mind, and of course Love, untrans-muted Love, flowing through that one, from the divine depth of that one.

The presence of Love in Form. Jeshua again.

How's the Viewpoint??
Well done.
Love to you all

Shamaré—The Guardian, the Protector, the Door Keeper, and the Gate Keeper

Addendum

Rightmindedness

Original notes:

'And so, here we are again, together.

As I move my attention and focus to you, I open myself to your needs at this moment and read you all.'

How did you get on with Spirituality 501?

Yes, a very big step it seems.

But now for the good part.

You are not alone in this quest—a concept or reality for you that you may have forgotten.

At the instant the belief in separation was being created, a side en-actment was also put in place by divine-source you, as a safety net.

Much as we do today in Ego—make a lifeboat or a way out of our creations, maybe a plane ticket so we can leave the scene rapidly if it turns upside down (smile).

All of Divine Source, God, All that is, did not fall into

separation, into dream; only the souls wanting to join.

Divine Source would not be God if this did not occur. It would be like suicide.

However, we put our hand up and said to the entity with the clipboard, 'Yes, include me please'.

But of course, in Reality we are multidimensional beings, and a piece of us remained safely intact in oneness and rightmindedness.

In truth, this rightmindedness is a composite of all, The Divine itself, and is therefore shared among all, as it originates from the only one thing that truly exists at all moments.

It is a pure spirit composite of all souls, undefiled and holy, and hence called Holy Spirit, or Divine Spirit. A dimension of True Self that is always available.

This one practises Holy or Divine Spirituality, or Whole Spirituality or Natural Spirituality or Original Birthed Spirituality or Holy Karma.

This energy of divinity is never lost and gives only loving guidance if called on. Ego is unknown to this energy; illusion and dream are impossible, only Oneness and Love flow from this one, that is Reality.

In truth, as you are one with all things and a composite of this, even in a dream state, you are linked to that one thing intimately also, pure Holy or Divine Spirit Energy.

It is abiding in you at all times and only needs to be reached out to, to have its guidance at any moment.

In fact, whenever you allow Love to flow to you and through you, from the depth of you, this is the action of this Holy or Divine Spirit, Pure Self or God Self.

So this is your True Pure Self, blessing your true pure self, who is asleep in an illusional dream, insane and living in an altered mind. That is all.

The blessing to you always, of course, is the call to awaken from the dream and withdraw from illusions and walk in and remember, 'Only Love again'.

So now be aware that what seemed like a selfless struggle can be shared or even surrendered to this energy.

Note: We say surrendered not about True Self, but about illusional self, the muddled, confusional self.

And so, my dear friends, now you can see the step to first Cause is made a little smoother and easier for the trans-formation and trans-cendence through the eye of the needle.

Some very important points now to gain success in your endeavours. You cannot fail. You can choose not to avail yourself of this. You can put the time off to do this. You can walk away shaking your metaphorical head. However, the curriculum is set and at some point the decision will be made to move through this to freedom divine.

A little preamble first.

We are talking about surrendering all, becoming empty of illusional self. Hence the need to practise flying right and learning to Love again.

To Love again is to Love Self again, by opening and allowing Love to flow through yourself again from the depth of you.

Loving Self leads to seeing that all is Self.

Until you have mastered this, no surrender can come. No healing, no change.

So let's ask a few questions to open this up more. Stop and do a check:

Are you getting pseudo joy and peace from being right about your beliefs?

Do you take pseudo pleasure from your beliefs?

Does it seem to give your life meaning?

Like being spiritual and others not?!

Good questions.

So now we are entering into a very interesting place in our discussion.

Your ego happiness and unhappiness are all the direct result of where you place your attention.

And if it is on a belief that is limiting or self-righteous or ??, this is ego tricking you into a place of being right and happy at the expense of others around you.

See how the discussion has moved now!

The definition of Effect is moving from not just re-activity, but also now to pleasure and being right and seemingly happy.

The subtleties of the ego are broad and endless, trapping the unaware every time.

Joy and Peace only come from Love flowing to you from the depth of you. There is no other way.

Everything else is a fabrication, a trick, a sleight of hand.

You cannot manage Love, you cannot contain it, you cannot make it.

Ego says it can do this and has a pseudo of this, a mimic love.

Jeshua says in 'A Course in Miracles' that one of the first creations of the Ego is the 'Face of Innocence'. This is the first piece you meet of an illusional self-creation in body, a projection of kindness, peace, pleasantness, even joy sometimes. Behind that face of innocence is everything that is dark and insane to keep the Ego intact.

You may have experienced this and asked how this can be several times by now.

They said they loved me. Their face of innocence was delightful, and now they have gone and they are saying hateful things about me. Where did the Love go all of a sudden? What happened to the Face of Innocence?

Well, there probably wasn't any Love there to start with. It was an ego projection, maybe of need or lust.

This is why all cultures developed a Face of Innocence. The great welcome, friendliness, hospitality. It is an ego mimic of Reality.

The ego cannot abide being seen as guilty, as not

having Love. It must put on a good show, only a projection out of fear of not having, so it makes a mimic.

That is why a seemingly Loving group of people, even a whole country, can suddenly drop the face of innocence and reveal great darkness and go to war against a neighbour.

And then return later and restore the face of innocence, and even apologize—or if the shame is too great, never mention it again.

So please do not get tricked into thinking that your behaviour is from Love flowing to you and through you at all times. It will be the 'Entrenched Face of Innocence' at work.

The Face of Innocence will drop when a complete surrender and allowance to the full trans-formation occurs, that is, the eye of the needle experience.

Notice when you are projecting; notice how you are managing your happiness and Joy. Notice when you step into The Face of Innocence. You will know. Welcoming someone you don't really want to welcome, forced smiling when you are being bullied, surrendering your sovereignty to a partner or work mate, or a multitude of things. It usually follows the thought, 'What will they think of me if I do not show the Face of Innocence to them?'

Sort of like a dog rolling over to have its tummy scratched.

Try this instead.

Take a breath and step back and say, 'I surrender the need to create, to look like I am Happy, Joyful, and Peaceful. It is not mine to make or create. It is a choice to allow, and it is a consequence of Love flowing through me and to me from the depth of me, only and always'.

I now open myself to Love flowing through me at this very moment.

My Joy and Peace is now complete always and forever. Amen—Be still.

You can get religious about this, but there is no need; it is just how it really is anyway.

But if the Amens and the holding together of hands and the bowing of the head and the closing of the eyes, if all that does something for you, then that is OK also until later.

The response that will now arise is something like this:

'You mean to say I have to take apart every facet of my life and rebuild it??'

Let's counter that with this question. Do you ever stop and ask by saying at any moment:

'Not my will be done (that is my ego will), but thy will (that is, the holy, divine, whole, loving one mind that is Real), be done.'

That is staying-in-Reality's will.

And of course, that is to stay in Joy, Peace, and Love flowing to you and through you from the depth of you, at every breath, every moment, every, every thought.

The other will is un-real and brings no Reality. Hence the strange results in life.

So the answer to your question: No rebuilding is required, but a surrender to your innocent true self is all that is required at any moment.

I am hoping by now this is starting to make an impression. This is quite another step.

I know you thought you just had to get rid of all the unhappy things and your life would be OK and full of meaning, Joy, Peace, and Love flowing through you.

Don't forget your happiness is also a fabrication if you are in ego mind.

And here is an interesting point. Have you noticed it is the unhappy bits that concern you the most? I just want to get rid of them, you probably say. I do not want to get rid of the things that are happy. What will I have left??

Yes, yes, it seems a dichotomy.

And so to make this process easier for you, I now want to introduce you to a new step in your game schedule with your life.

This is just to try on, and it is not serious. Make it a fun thing to do.

Notice if you have a conversation with someone in which you have a discussion about your knowing and being right, when there is general agreement and pleasantness and maybe a laugh or two. At the end of this communication, or later, rework the event in your mind.

Ask yourself, 'Would I re-word this communication, would I change anything?' and allow yourself to see that it may be just a projection of ego that took place. 'Was I talking beliefs as if they were totally true?'

And so, you can now see the game has opened up

even more, and we are in 501 Addendum. (Will this ever stop?? You would expect a big finale. There is more yet.)

And if that is not enough for you—yes heap it on, I am strong now, you say. Smile.

Grievance with anyone must be healed and dropped. It is with yourself only.

It is quite simple. If you have a grievance you are projecting and declaring the other as guilty, and of course in the same thought you convict yourself of the same crime.

You, who were created by Love, can hold no grievance and Know Self. To hold a grievance is to forget who you are. To hold a grievance is to see yourself as body only. To hold a grievance is to let the ego rule your mind and to condemn yourself to death. It immediately splits you off from Source, God, All that is Self, and makes you unlike that One. (ACIM)

Death here being not knowing Full Reality Life.

And that splitting off includes Holy Divine Spirit Self. You lock yourself out from the grand helper that is trying to find ways to be of help always.

So now is an excellent time to start to examine for grievance with others around you, not just for them, but for yourself. This whole thing is very selfish, divinely selfish.

Go through the ones you may have a grievance with, and go see them if they are close; write an email if far. Say, 'I want you to know I am moving on and setting you free from my judgment'. A hug. They may laugh or cry, but in truth, you set yourself free from your own guilt and judgment at that moment.

You can see we are mopping up around the edges of our grand dream now, getting it all out of the way.

You are well enough along to hear this sort of information. Imagine if you were told at the beginning about the Face of Innocence and the need to drop the fabrication of happiness.

So you can see, you have moved your mind well along now and are accepting of more and more change, allowance, and surrender. Loosening up, as it were. Shaking off the entanglements.

And remember this: you are not really learning anything new. What can be new?

Moving into simplicity, as was discussed at the beginning.

So entering the eye of the needle is the quest.

You may have to do forty days and nights in a desert (smile).

Actually, your life now is your forty days and forty nights. It is all very metaphorical, don't you feel? See how far you can push that metaphor.

And so the eye of the needle:

You will find it is a natural flow. Open yourself to all help; declare your innocence of—

Not knowing what a single thing is or what it is really for.

The dropping to the knees metaphorically, the surrender.

Teach me anew. I am now a willing candidate.

And this is every moment, every breath, every thought or after every thought also.

Teach me anew, correct my mind. I am an open book to be examined.

You will know you are in the path to the eye of the needle if all this is going on and only Love is flowing to you and through you from the depth of you. Your total focus. Your new Viewpoint.

Anything else and you are just kidding yourself. You

will know if you are kidding yourself, as simplicity will go and complexity will rise up once again.

There is a tendency also in some to want to seem holy or knowing more.

Drop it. Laugh at that one.

Burn the paraphernalia, the crosses, the gowns, the smokers, the incense, the false smile, the condescension, the outward symbols of holiness, as you burn the inside paraphernalia also.

It will all happen naturally anyway.

And so we now enter into silence and allow the flow of all good things to continue.

I hope you are in the swing, as they say.

If you get stuck and you can't seem to shake it, ask self or ask a friend!

Original Notes again.

'There will be one more communication chapter in this series, and then we will leave this until the next arising thought of communication.'

May you discover Your Inner Peace, and that your life becomes full of Joy as Love flows endlessly to you and through you from the depth of you.

You are not alone, and much help is available at all moments.

Become truly helpful: Teach all "Only Love is Real"—by living this.

How's the Viewpoint??
Well done.
Love to you all

Shamaré—The Guardian, the Protector, the Door Keeper, and the Gate Keeper

Spirituality 601

You Are the True Cause and Effect

Original Notes again.

This Spirituality 601 chapter will conclude the formal discussion on Awakening from the Dream of the Dreamer.

However, I have been encouraged to continue to offer practical help and add some other documentation for you after this chapter.

This practical help will include some mind healing work done with one of the readers, as they learned to apply love to healing long-time recurring habits, issues, or re-activity.

And so to conclude this communication in a way of help for you, we need to enter into Reality itself.

Oops, we are already there; we just need to re-focus our attention in this (smile).

So take a deep breath and say, 'I now move my

attention into Reality itself'. Breathe out and relax into it.

Much of the discussion so far has been how to seemingly heal inside a non-reality, that is the ego mind and inside your ego creations.

And of course you can't heal a non-reality, but you can dissolve from the mind the cause and hence the ongoing effect.

We are now going to work from a position of Reality itself and work inside this Reality.

Actually you always do. It just seems otherwise.

Inside Reality, you have just added fear, guilt, and judgment components that build virtuality and madness, and this disturbs your natural Joy and Peace. And with this disturbance every now and then you stop Love flowing to and through you, from the depth of you.

This stopping of Love is caused by the belief that there is separation from True Self and your self (ego). Impossible, of course, as Love only flows from you to yourself. And if separation did exist, you would cease to be in an instant.

So inside Reality we will work with as much disconnection from ego as we have.

The mind healing work we will do this time is outside beliefs and outside so-called knowledge or information learnt in some way.

This Spirituality 601 section is linking all the pieces together from all the previous chapters. The focus so far has been on several key points.

Ego Cause and Effect and using Love flowing from Reality to heal the Ego Causes as we tunnel inside Ego Effects. The Ego Effect window, doorway, or gateway and the emotional tunnel always lead to an Ego Cause or Causes.

And so, we have discussed Ego Cause and Effect for some time now, and slowly brought to the surface of the mind this idea of you being the Creator of all things for you, so it is accessible and understood by you.

By now you will have worked out that Cause and Effect inside Ego is not real at all, as anything inside Ego is unreal or just a creation based on concepts, ideas, beliefs, learnings, etc.

It is as a dream you have carefully made.

A thought arises, 'I would like to experience this outcome', and there it is for you. Maybe not right away, but over time you genuinely create the world you seem to live in.

You will also have worked out by now that when I mentioned, 'Here is a new concept for you', that this was to appeal to Ego mind, as Ego likes concepts, so-called knowledge, and learning.

However, in Reality there is no need for concepts or beliefs. Reality just is. No struggle, no learning, no books, no authority, only Love flowing to you and through you, with all sacred knowledge available and equality of this knowledge for all as one.

And it all arises from the depth of you! Freely and available always, as the natural. No learning.

Concepts are only that—ideas, thoughts, beliefs, or imaginings, a way to explain to an ego mind, maybe a learning process.

So to reiterate, in Reality there is no need for such things, as Reality is sure and solid and dependable and unchanging.

Just like you.

You remain unchanged, unchanging, and unchangeable forever, even now as you may be struggling to drop the ego identification. Ego is not permanent. It is fluid and dissolves with Love.

You are the rock this whole thing is built upon; we all are. You will see why in a few more lines.

However, just for a little light entertainment, we can use Ego Cause and Effect (Ego Karma) as a useful teaching tool at this juncture, since we are so familiar with it now.

Using this concept or idea, we can now swing across into Reality and see and understand, maybe for the first time, that inside Reality itself there is also Real Cause and Real Effect operating, Real Karma.

Yes, we are using Ego Cause and Effect as just a metaphor for Reality itself. A little cheeky touch.

Knowing that a Real Cause and Real Effect operates does take the sting out of small, unreal Ego cause and effect a little, doesn't it?

So to get grounded thoroughly in Reality, let's introduce this idea again.

In Truth and Reality there is only one thing turning, the Universe, and it is only Spiritual, it is Loving energy, and all components of it are interconnected as one. You reside there always.

The whole Universe is operating in the One Mind, the One Love, the One Cause.

Yes, now you can see Love is the real Cause from Divine Source itself, and it flows endlessly from the depth of you. You are connected to Divine Source

Cause directly; there is no separation ever. Never has been.

Real Cause flows to you individually from the great creating mystery and source of all things, every moment. It always has for you.

Life itself springs from this Cause for you. The cloning of you in that image is as it is for all souls, individuated, mirrors of the one energy itself. God spurning god or the one Cause making Effects though many souls, thus God experiencing god endlessly and continually.

And just as you automatically, when in ego mind, respond to your each and every moment of Cause with much Effect (drama and suffering and acting), so it is true with Real Cause.

It is just opening to this and letting go of Ego the Self-Identification that seems to drive a wedge between you and Source or Reality itself.

Another way to say this and it will show a little of your own history behind these words:

Just as you have been devoted to your Ego, placing all your attention and waking hours on this created mechanism, this idol, this worship, your altar; now you can place all your devotion on Reality itself.

The day has come when all will worship the Divine

father or mother in Spirit and Truth. Now doesn't that change the meanings behind those ancient words spoken to the Samaritan women at the well?

You have had great desire, intention, and allowance for Ego, with full surrender, being vigilant for the self-identified person you created in error.

You probably were prepared to fight or even die for the devotion.

The same is true in Reality. Just a shift of Attention. The New Viewpoint.

Hence all those little props along the way in these discussions, to lead and turn the mind to Reality.

In contrasting the two Causes, Ego and Reality, all things suddenly jump into focus.

When you are in Surrender to Reality, Divine Cause is accepted as authority; it is automatic and natural, just as it is in illusional Ego devotion. In fact, it is easier in Divine Cause, due to no confusion, no fear, no guilt, no need to be right, and judging everything.

Maybe this will be your response to this contrasting view—

Oh my goodness me.

I have been missing Real Cause all this time.

It was as if I was blind to this.

I was so blinkered.

I was only thinking my Ego Cause was right and essential.

I thought I had to fight or be clever, to make my purpose true and real.

How could I have been so blind to have missed this Real Cause?

The Dream was just that—a sleep with many illusions.

Also a great deal of struggle and insanity.

There was no awareness of Reality, only glimpses now and then and hope in the deeper moments of despair and insanity.

Maybe in silent prayer when things looked grim.

This new Realisation makes complete sense and removes all the dichotomies and confusion on all things.

I now hear you saying:

I forgive myself for ever thinking My Way was ever right.

My Own Will led me to dreams.

I forgive myself for ever thinking there was no Real Love.

I forgive myself for all the illusions and drama I have created for myself.

And, as I move my attention from being stuck on my created Ego Cause (My Way) to Real Cause (The One Way), I open to Love flowing to me and through me from the depth of me, to heal all things.

I surrender to this new Cause and delight in the Awareness that has arisen in me.

I am made anew.

Now that I have surrendered, I have left the dream and entered into Reality itself.

And, my oh my, I am already here.

And as Real Cause motivates me, I see and become aware of it, my True Purpose.

Yes, yes, I am in Truth—Real Effect in operation.

And how could this not ever be true. Only in dreams.

I am the Real Effect now.

My Purpose is to allow Cause—Love flowing to me and through me, from the Divine depth of me—to motivate me and move me to be loving in all situations I am led to.

I am the true manifestation of the original creative purpose from Divine Source or God or Love.

God motivating god to expand Love in a myriad of ways.

I now open to this new will, True Cause, which is now my own True Will, that is flowing in Harmony with all Real Things.

The Real Effect is me acting Lovingly all the time, automatically without prompting or thought.

I delight, we delight, in bringing forth more and more Love to any place where we find ourselves.

All those words now take on a fuller meaning.

You are the Light of the world.

You are the one you have been searching for all this time.

You are Love itself.

You are the way, the truth, and the life, of course. And much more.

Now you can see why I can say even before you knew and understood this, it is all true for you.

And you doubted.

I am sure now you can see this is the only harmony that is truly possible.

And here is something I am sure you have wondered about also: how giving Love away as you receive it multiples it.

Well, the only difference between the two Causes and Effects is this. The Ego or unreal Cause is nothing and can be Loved away at any moment. Real Cause, Love flowing to you, cannot be loved away with Love, it can only enhance it or be multiplied.

The more you fall into Love and breathe it, the more there is.

It would be like trying to eradicate the mystery of yourself or God itself or Love, and that is not a possibility ever.

So how about that?!

Get your head in that, as you would say, and see the only thing that is required at any moment is to say, 'I surrender to Love itself and drop all other things'.

Breathe in and let out with intention and a smile.

Hence Jeshua's thoughts, even after 2000 years, become our thoughts.

'Give me more of this, give me more and more, ceaselessly, ever more, ever expanding, ever more loving'.

Surrender is only a step away.

To expand on this, to give a greater depth of meaning to it all, another way to describe Real Effect is working inside Christ Mind.

Yes, you can see that immediately.

Hence Christ Spirit as Jeshua was Emmanuel. With us is God!

Christ Mind is our play area for all Cause that comes to us.

And hence when you do surrender, you become the Return of Christ itself.

Not the return of Jesus or Jeshua, but as the Effect, running in Christ Mind.

And how powerful is that?!

True Cause motivating 1,000 or 100,000 souls who dwell in Christ Mind as Real Effect is a powerful force.

A Co-Creation of Power that will bring Heaven to Earth, not with force but with Love and healing of all minds back to Real Cause and Effect. Holy Karma in action.

So now you can feel comfortable about the outcome.

No interventions, no chariots of fire and retribution, etc.

It is just a choice that will be made at some point by any and all.

You can make your choice now or soon.

And so you become The Way, the Truth, and the Life.

See how that fits more comfortably now.

Amazing, and many of you almost vomited when you heard those words some time back.

Breathe and smile.

You have become the Saviour of the world.

Another one for many, where you would say, 'Bring me a bucket' when you heard words like this.

Well, you have been through very much, and much has been judged as destructive and harmful to freedom, hence it was just an Ego knee jerk reaction (effect) and an emphatic way to put some distance between you and the old religious ideas that you had worked through and rejected and judged.

I forgive myself for this judgment. It was an effect that brewed up inside me.

And old guilt of how I used to be at some point along the road.

Smile on that, it has no lasting effects.

Original Notes:

I am blank at this point of writing, awaiting Cause to move my mind again to complete this for us all.

In closing then: And so it is done—101 to 601.

A very short version of many other endeavours. A miracle.

Nevertheless, it has focused the mind back to Truth and Reality.

Those that have read my larger work, 'A Course in Miracles' (ACIM), will recognise the many parallels and expansions and subtle completions.

For those listening to 'The Way of the Heart' recordings, this information is helpful in that it condenses or shortens Time.

It seems in most cases, you need to know before you can know.

Have you noticed that now?

Read all of this again and see the conclusion is well defined, and go back if you need to ACIM and 'The Way of the Heart' as reference or comfort, maybe as a soother.

It is, however, just more of the same.

Do not get stuck in ritualising information! It is a very common trap.

Better yet, isn't it time to slide across the divide in your mind gently to Reality permanently?

Next chapter will be an epilogue with more encouragement.

Be gentle on yourselves, and when doubt or self-incrimination comes up, stop, breathe, fall into it and forgive yourself, as it is just an old idea or habit trying to slow you down.

When I say sit in it, it may not require stopping working or doing. You may find you can still do all of that easy stuff and still sit in a non-judgmental manner inside the emotions and watch and smile and slowly slide into Peace with it all. Try it on for size.

Realisations will come. Healing will come.

Sometimes you may need to sit inside this for several weeks.

Just do it and learn to observe your mind. Yes, buckle under to the prompting by Spirit to drop all other things from major focus and just sit in it all, the swirl of emotions.

You can carry on working, smiling, helping, loving, and sharing. You can do this all at the same time as sitting in surrender.

Remember it took me, Jeshua Ben Joseph, many, many years to finally crack the puzzle and step into True Ownership and Self Love, and the rest is history.

I had much help along the way, great parents that supported me, financed me, loved me. I met all the great teachers of the time, all over the ancient world, even as far afield as England and India.

My return to Palestine was a mystery to me that unfolded, as it is right now.

I do not push the parcel as it is said, I allow, I surrender, I smile and have delight as it opens.

And it took me, as Shamaré, much focused effort and much searching, going down seemingly many wrong roads, to finally reach this point of discussion with you all.

Much learning, books, travelling, gurus and teachers, religions, -isms and -ologies, to finally realise that Only Love is Real.

However, it is complete and there is no turning back to dreams when you know what we all know now.

There is a vast array of help available to you.

Just ask at any moment.

I ask for help this moment.

And it is there, breathe and go still.

How could it be otherwise!

And also you can be this vast array of help, by just so slightly changing your attention and focus.

Try it on for size by saying, 'I am offering myself as help from now on. It is true now'.

You will work with many who come to you, silently via mind connection.

You will feel them, you will ask 'who are you', and you will know.

You will be able to hold a mind in pain, effect and cause, remotely it would seem, and allow them to heal themselves.

And with that, we will end this chapter.

The Grand and yes Holy Cause and Effect of the Universe.

How's the Viewpoint??
Well done.
Love to you all

Shamaré—The Guardian, the Protector, the Door Keeper, and the Gate Keeper

Spirituality Epilogue

This chapter will offer some summary to the full 101 to 601 discussion, with a few extra insights.

We hope you have en-Joyed the journey into words and concepts and that you once again are now using your feelings to unlock the doors to true freedom, as you surrender your attention from Ego identification of being body back to identification of True Self as Spirit.

The change of Viewpoint.

The return to Spirituality is about recognising you are Spirit and once again trusting the invisible.

Quite a step.

It is about the True and only form we all are, as one.

Spirituality is about existence as Spirit and the use of the one vehicle to experience this existence, the One Mind with no Separation.

A soul whose mind is spiritually centred will be fully aware, crystal clear and vast, with only Love, Joy, and Peace in that mind as the driving energy.

In Truth and Reality, that is how it is always, except for when you have allowed the mind to enter into fearful dreams or mis-perceptions.

This Peace and Joy is our birthright state and truly is our only mental state until we allow other self-created non-Love energies to dominate for a short while. A mutation of Love takes place.

The experiment/game of separation is exactly that, a clouded mind with a section of mind seemingly under control by fear, guilt, and judgments, some of the time. This is a choice.

These energies are a self-construct, a self-creation, a trans-mutation of Love, a choice into aberration, a move into illusion, and an allowing of insanity in which the dream of the dreamer is experienced, especially if you take it all seriously. You could laugh them away and your attention would not get stuck.

However, it is seriousness that captures the fear-mutated energy and holds it in place. So a good idea is to loosen up a little each day.

Spirituality is just one word, a title, a label, and it tries to convey an infinite experience. Very difficult indeed, especially when you consider the word is propagated to ego mind identified inside a creation outside Reality itself.

However it does offer a differentiation from similar ideas, such as religion, meditation, other -isms and -ologies, etc.

Words are symbols of symbols, twice removed from reality. (ACIM)

To reach Reality as an experienced state requires climbing back up the symbols.

First, the word Spirituality. A dictionary will give the meaning and an intellectual understanding of this word, and you decide if you want to experience what is conveyed inside its meaning.

The word Spirituality is defined by a series of other words (more symbols) that try to give some idea of the experience. Hence twice removed from that reality.

Second, the words in the definition try to convey Ideas or Thoughts of Spirituality.

Does this idea or thought resonate with something you know in other thoughts and ideas? Do you remember ancient thoughts and ideas? Does it bring you through to a mental position where you want to experience these ideas and thoughts? One step from Reality.

Third, the experiential events of Spirituality, that is, the return to Reality itself.

At this Reality level you know the words, thoughts, and ideas in infinite ways, through feelings and direct experiences. You can taste it, rather than talk or think about it.

The vast landscape of Spirituality opens to you.

This does mean then—feeling and experience are everything. Books, words, and ideas are only signposts, pointing to experience. There is little progress just knowing intellectually.

The awakening process is therefore a feeling process and an awareness practice that must be entered into and held at all moments.

The stepping into Spirituality requires leaving Ego mind behind. This small part of the mind that is seemingly overrun with fear is described by Jeshua as the cesspool of denial.

Harsh words, it seems at first, but also very apt to gain people's mental attention who are inside Ego.

The question arises, 'What is better?'

Ego is literally full of mental waste and is a smelly place, with all sorts of drama and denial that take away Joy and Peace. Love stops flowing!

Our 101 to 601 discussion was about the journey leading back to clarity or purity of the one mind once again where that mind runs in harmony with the one energy, the one Love.

The 101–601 project is therefore a recovery of Mind.

Spirituality and Mind go hand in hand. Mind is where it is experienced.

The journey is also deeply personal and comes only as your willingness allows you to forgive mis-perceptions and denials that do not serve you, and this forgiveness allows a Peaceful, Joyful state of Mind to return.

This process does take some time. So use time constructively. Do not waste time.

In all situations know and apply this, that Love allows, trusts, embraces, trans-forms, trans-cends, and trans-mutes all things outside of Love, back to Love itself.

A miracle in the small myopic mind of the Ego, but totally understood inside Reality.

To be outside of Love, all those situations must be un-real or a mis-creation, a mistake in thought and attention or a mis-understanding.

Another way to say this is, and it may help:

God allows, trusts, embraces all things, and we as

the agent extensions of the mystery of god itself, can only ever mimic that one energy.

Does that help?

There is nothing else possible. It is a choiceless choice unless you want to shake yourself free from Reality itself, and we all know that is impossible.

Some choose dreams instead.

To counter dreams, taking up a spiritual practice is a wise thing to do, especially if you are stuck in your dreams somewhere and desire to return home to Joy and Peace.

Another way to say this is to return to heavenly bliss, which is not a place as such but a state of mind, and that means you can be in any dimension or domain in Reality itself and remain in Bliss.

Does that help?

Even on a little ball spinning in space somewhere, controlling a body but knowing you are inseparable from Spirit itself.

So along the mental journey home, please do enJoy each self-discovery and the release of misperception and denial.

Actually relish each and every moment that comes

to you, as an opportunity to move your awareness back to home. For that is what you are doing each time you shed light and Love over yourself.

The act of Self Love is the journey home, as without Self Love there is no return to Peace or Joy. Love heals all things. Only Love. Nothing else works.

You are the prodigal child returning back home to celebration after a long journey full of great experiences and troubles.

The gateway to recognising Spirit again is via the mind. Open the mind to all things, allow all your mis-creations to dance for you, and you may then release them, as a child releases toys when they become older.

All experience is only of the mind.

You created the world you see. It is a mirror of your mind for you, as there is nothing outside of you at any level.

Use this mirror that reflects back to you all your mental perceptions, all of your mind at work.

This is all you can ever see and understand in Ego. The mirror is you in action mentally. Wow!

Use this mirror to observe yourself.

There is nothing else that will teach you as quickly or personally, as only you can recognise your own creations and release them, forgiving yourself as you go down the path to freedom.

You can go to endless classes and study, read endless books about healing and spirituality, but nothing beats getting into a pair of gumboots and wading into the mud and getting dirty in the middle of a big puddle of mis-perception and denial.

This is what happens when you look out of your eyes and listen with your ears and start to heal all the goings-on that reflect back to you, your errors.

Jeshua says it this way:

Your life, your very life, is the best ashram in the world. Each lesson in this ashram is tailored directly and closely, in fact exactly for you and no one else.

You cannot have better or closer attention to your needs in your spiritual practice each and every moment.

The game of flying right into re-activity or mis-perception is just that, practise, until you have unwound yourself enough to start to hear again the still, clear voice of your source energy.

This grand mystery of all things, talking and encouraging you once again.

Whispering to you, 'Awaken child, you are already home, it was only a dream'.

Listen to this voice; it is your direction home.

Say something like this to open yourself to this:

'I open myself to myself at a deeper level and ask for correction to come to me.'

There will be no condemnation, only help, only Love and then the opening of the mind for your next step to freedom, the next forgiving of yourself of this set of mis-perceptions and denials you have just been made aware of.

This will become your pre-occupation eventually. Each and every moment you will seek direction automatically, without a fight.

Fear will not raise its head after a while.

As Love grows in you, you will just fall into a natural default state of waiting for direction, not from someone outside of you, like a God that sits on a throne somewhere, but the god that is inside you and is intimately part of you.

'I surrender each moment to the direction coming to me from the depths of my depths.'

It is relatively easy and requires just a pinch of willingness to start and continue.

Move from living life re-actively with mis-perception, to living life directly or deliberately, consciously. That is being aware of what is happening and knowing where it all flows from.

Stopping the making of mud puddles and at some point taking off the gumboots and relaxing deeply into yourself once again.

True purpose is revealed as it becomes very clear you are nothing but Effect, a window or a doorway to allow Love out into wherever you happen to be.

You are driven by the depths of Cause itself, a mystery of infinity that Loves you and has made you.

Inside the One thing, all is harmony and filled with great happiness and contentment.

And if you find yourself still attached to a body on a planet called Earth spinning somewhere, you drop into that mode of delivering Love in this domain, as a bee goes around pollinating flowers.

You shower Love into this creation, not by being

good and nice but by being the presence of love itself.

What will be required of you is not your concern, you just ask.

'What would you have me express?'

'Oh, Heaven on Earth, oh my goodness what a great idea.'

'I bless the earth and all that is in it.'

And of course the bringing of heaven to earth is only a mental state that must be achieved by a great number of like-minded souls in harmony.

Maybe not even talking to one another or knowing one another in a physical way but resonating the same song of Love.

Heaven on Earth, as Jeshua says, is an illusion, but it is at least a happy illusion.

Because how is it possible to bring Reality to a non-reality?

Well, it will be a blast seeing it unfold, as the final part of the dream, this time in a conscious state, an aware state.

And after that, well it is a while away, and the physical creation is only hung on one thought.

And with that, we will leave you to ponder and imagine the outcome.

Walking in Reality (or as Jeshua likes to call it, 'The Kingdom') is another matter.

We can explore that together when the time comes.

Actually, it will be outside time and in a place of infinity.

Now, we are not complete yet, as there are some more little things to do for us all.

Next will be a short (or not so short) dictionary, and then after that a short but powerful example of how one healed a piece of their mind, and you might find you are part of the same story.

Now to all those that have expressed their gratitude for these short but poignant chapters, we thank you, but more importantly, it is a grand sign you have all of this inside yourself already and it is resonating, even begging to come out. So thank yourself, you asked for them, yes really.

So ask yourself this question.

What can I do for myself right now and every now, to help bring heaven to earth?

And the bushel basket must be consigned to the furnace, finally, after these 2000 years of waiting.

All of creation and those that support it are waiting for this day to be.

Some would hope it comes as a chariot of fire and destroys all the baddies (smile).

I think Jeshua has one parked in his garage waiting. However, it was a surprise to see a herd of reindeers out the back (smile).

Some would stand on a hilltop with up-stretched hands waiting for rapture (smile).

Some hope when the body takes its last breath they will enter into bliss (smile).

We know it is just a decision away.

'I choose this moment to enter into bliss itself' (and laugh).

How could you fail unless you choose to stop it?

Remember it is your mind, and no one can subvert it other than you.

So Love to you all.

You may ask questions if you like, and we can drop

them before the council of the high priests of the ascended masters (and they will then laugh also).

And if you feel stuck and immobile mentally at any time, cry out.

'I feel stuck and immobile, I desire correction and healing to come to me and it is done.'

And if you don't believe it will come, cry out.

'I feel it will not come, I desire correction and healing to come to me and it is done.'

You see how it works.

At some point you will break it open and move forward.

May Peace of Mind overcome you entirely and you become finally at ease.

How's the Viewpoint??
Well done.
Love to you all

Shamaré—The Guardian, the Protector, the Door Keeper, and the Gate Keeper

Spirituality Dictionary

Part I

You are the dictionary itself, as you personally ascribe meaning to all events, thoughts, words, ideas, and even the grand emotions that are a part of your experience, based on your perception and the value you place on any events.

This does mean one thing: you define your life itself and make all meaning you know, and it comes true for you.

This also means your experience is individuated by you, and it seems unique, doesn't it?

Two people eating the same apple will say in words, it is tart, sweet, bitter, crunchy, etc., but who is ever to know exactly what either of them actually mean or feel?

Only a general outline of meaning is possible, and by group agreement we can say that ice cream is yummy, especially rum and raisin or chocolate, if you seem to live in a human body, in some particular culture or country or domain or age.

That would be true possibly for humans, but maybe dogs or elephants would see it differently.

So you can see, a dictionary with all definitions is a grand project and will be fraught with inconsistencies and generalities.

Therefore, experience rather than definition in symbols is always far superior in every way.

Words or symbols and ideas and thoughts are but a blurred facsimile of experience.

And when you are clear in mind, you can actually broadcast that experience to others for them to experience also.

Oh yes, in fact you do this regularly without seeming to know, and they are receiving the transmission, especially those linked to you and those that love you.

And so with these limits in mind, we will try to be helpful with some word symbol definitions and in most cases add a short discussion on each word, to elucidate more understanding.

Does it ever strike you odd that Humanity loves

looking at little picture symbols or alphabet squiggles and take meaning from it?

A big part of human life is dedicated to mastering this feat! Smile.

And then a lifetime of using them to try and describe experience and things. Yes, labels for the contrivances. LOL.

Never before have humans devoted more time to reading and viewing symbols, especially on handheld devices connected to the greatest array of symbols via a broad communication system.

To set the stage again:

There are some Spiritual and Ego terms that are not commonly used and these need a little explaining, especially for the student embarking or just starting for the first time on a spiritual journey.

Better to have a general idea of the meaning of word symbols and yes, sound symbols, than to guess.

A good teacher always knows their audience and will adapt communication appropriately. The choice of words in that communication is important.

When you first meet a spiritual teacher who

teaches 'Only Love is Real', there is usually a vocabulary used to describe the Ego–Spiritual divide.

The meanings in this vocabulary often turn everything the student ever knew on its head and can be a little disconcerting for the student at first.

Exclamations are often heard, sometimes in a whisper, so as not to appear foolish or unknowing in front of the guru (smile).

I don't understand that.

It does seem hard to grasp

and even,

How can this be possible or true??

A clash of dictionaries and meanings.

A laugh and a smile will set the path straight again.

A few of these words that can cause confusion for new students or are seldom used are listed now.

Spirituality
Ego
Reality
World
Creation
Illusion

Insanity
Duality
Awareness
Consciousness
Time
Projection
Denial
Expectation
Mirror
Perception
Belief
Soul
Body
Matter
Spirit
Trans-formation
Trans-cendence
Trans-mutation
Effect
Cause

Also a couple of phrases that may not make a lot of sense at first:

You don't know what a single thing is and what it is for.

and

There is nothing outside of you.

And then a host of words used in Ego talk that will need some further consideration as you move to a spiritual life.

A re-consideration of meaning and use of:

Guilt
Judgment
Fear
Separation
Vulnerable
Victim
Stuck
Denial
Anger
Confusion
Shock
Excessive Joy
Unresponsive
Disgust
Low Self-Esteem
Grief
Irritated
Resentful

Also some little word whiskers:

But
Should
Could

Would
Because
If only

There is also a long list of sub words that spin off from the major emotion list, which try to further capture the nuances of the emotion and feelings.

We will leave these to your own explanation and meaning, arising from connection with Reality itself.

From our 101 to 601 exploration into Spirit, we can say that the Ego-trained intellectual mind has almost no part in the True Mind healing process, and even less in true understanding of Spirit.

True Intelligence, in contrast to Ego Intellect, is inherent and part of our birthright as Children of the Mystery and the Light, and it is not a learned function. It is accessible equally by all souls.

At a human level, this intelligence is sometimes masked or denied.

That does not mean it is not there, just a soul is choosing to play world dualities in a certain format for a while.

On awakening, intelligence is part of the effect you become, progressively opening and allowing, surrendering into the Source of all Mystery's Cause as guide.

Spirituality can therefore be described as a soul opening to the invisible source of intelligence in the universe and living in a deep, unbroken, moment-by-moment relationship with that intelligence.

Living connected and in harmony to Reality itself always.

This is true in all domains, from 3rd dimensional space and time to the highest states of spirit possible. No GAP.

Ego is a choice made to pretend to live outside of this intelligence and mask out this intelligence and live from a defined identification other than Spirit. Usually a body, but not always.

Ego is a separated, self-defined illusionary viewpoint and is outside Reality.

Hence it is a creation and can be said to be based on a mis-perception or mis-understanding of Reality.

As it is outside Reality, it can also be said to not really exist; it is a dream and has no effect on true existence.

When any mind thinks that it is the definition the Ego ascribes, and this is then taken seriously and the definition is believed real and correct, that mind falls into insanity.

A final descriptor is that Ego is actually Hell to try to live in. The mental hell is believing it is cut off from source itself.

Reality is permanent, where we all truly reside as Spirit always. We cannot leave this mental domain, which has a default energy of Love, Joy, allowing a fully Peaceful Mind.

It is inside Reality that consciousness and awareness only ever exist. Reality is unchanging, unchanged, and unchangeable and has a playground called the One Mind where all activity takes place.

Inside Reality, all are connected as One, bound by family relationship, same energy, same resonance.

World is, first of all, not the planet Earth. There are many worlds, world within worlds, and they exist as illusions in Ego minds only as creations.

These worlds represent a thought or idea in action as a creation. There can be groups in general agreement on how these worlds should, could, and would run. Mass consciousness in Ego mind, a grouping, a culture, a nation, a species.

Creation is a projection of a thought from mind to spiritually make or accomplish something.

The act of creating is fundamental to all Souls and goes on ceaselessly in all domains.

An example of creation is the Ego mind, and hence a world and also worlds inside worlds, a complexity.

Creations are not Reality and therefore are only sustained by a thought or thoughts that started the creation process.

In most cases they are only a virtualisation or a mimic, and can be a metaphor for Reality.

E.g., Human families and relationships through bodies.

Illusions are often the end result of creations taken seriously.

An illusion is a substitute or mimic creation that, if taken seriously, almost always leaves the creator feeling disconnected from reality.

Thus also a delusion or a mind that has lost objectivity.

Insanity is the end result of illusions, as there seems to be a disconnect from reality.

Ego mind is entirely insane in all aspects.

Duality perception is the result of the idea and the thought and then the subsequent creation of, 'What would it be like to live in a world where there is not only love?'

Instantly inside this new illusionary perception was the possibility that 'Only Love is Real' may not be true.

Inside this illusion, the opposite is also possible.

Hence a duality of outcomes or possibilities.

This start point led to a world of dualities, the goods and bads, rights and wrongs, moral or immoral, godly or not godly, or simply any two bands of energies in contra corners, rather than the one energy of Love flowing with Joy, Peace of Mind, and Innocence.

Awareness To know or perceive.

Consciousness A mental state that allows an understanding and knowledge and experience of the arising Loving Mystery that flows through us all. Life itself.

It allows the experience of Self or individuated Soul.

This experience is only ever in the One mind at Spirit level.

Consciousness exists in all souls, whether as spirit or spirit experiencing any incarnation, such as being human or something else.

Anything arising from Source is imbued with Consciousness.

A little more might be helpful: In humanity there is seeming consciousness; however it is still arising nowhere but in the mind in 5th dimension and above.

So when a human body seems to lose consciousness, this is just a drop in the communication link and not really loss of consciousness per se.

This link in most cases is recovered, and the experience of soul being human (smile on that) is restored.

Much like at so-called body death—same phenomenon. No loss of consciousness, just a drop of the comms link to a body and moving the attention back to spirit.

That will help immeasurably.

Time A creation mechanism and a projection into the physical universe.

As Spirit or in Reality, there is no time, hence timelessness.

The phrase 'At the End of Time' is exactly that. Time can end and will on our agreement.

Time is held in place by an agreed group thought, just as is the physical universe.

If this group thought is released, so is Time and Physicality.

Physicality and Time are the Effect of the Cause thought. >>>Yes

Many Egoic writings would have you believe that the end of time is Conflagration Time.

It is just the end of the game for physicality, bodies, space and time; life as Spirit continues with arising new creations, moment by moment, never ending.

Projection A discovered ability of mind at some point.

It is a mechanism of creation. A thought arises and a projection of mind allows the creation.

In Ego mind, projection still works. It is used as

a tool for unloading fear, guilt, and judgment at others.

An ego thought arises from mis-perception, such as, 'This is a fearful situation; I feel insecure and I am losing ego sovereignty, so I must unload this somehow. I will project this out as anger or frustration at someone else, or I will have a hissy-fit as a major drama, or break down and cry, or strike out'.

It is a major tool used in ego relationships to shift blame, fear, anger, etc. From couple relationships to group, to nation relationships that end in conflict, these are all projections. War.

Denial An old Egyptian habit.

A decision to ignore or pretend to not know or be responsible for.

At any moment when a soul says they are not responsible for their projection or creation, it is a denial.

In Ego configurations of mind, this happens continually. It is in every mode of the life as a body.

I just got all emotional, but they incited me, they are responsible.

I am body, I am not spirit.

I cannot control myself, I am addicted.

I am stupid and dumb.

Etc.

All denials of who you really are.

Taking responsibility and dropping denial is the beginning of healing.

Enough of the dictionary for the moment.

This is a three-part series.

However, I am being encouraged to talk a little in closing this section, with a discussion on Communication.

The 'Moment interface of each relationship and communication' is a knotty area where the inability to express ideas and thoughts to the other is often a limiting factor in attaining intimacy and transparency and oneness with that one.

Hence the Ego's major project is to educate, to seemingly overcome this.

Does it work? Well, history and herstory tells a different story.

However, by now it is most certainly obvious that

one of the biggest limitations in communication is mis-perceptions and beliefs.

And even worse, if there are degrees (in Ego there are), the lack of ability to connect to emotions directly sometimes makes communication a little woody or shut down.

Hence the feminine with their often greater ability with emotions are often asking for better communication from masculine partners.

And this encouragement is well worth listening to.

It is, however, at the interface of your relationship with self and self that great gains can be made in this area of communication.

That is, clearing up what you really mean when you say something to self. Setting yourself straight.

You will recall back at the beginning of Spirituality 101 that Self Dialogue was encouraged, and now it is about to be expanded for you to join in.

To listen to Self speaking healing words even to Ego mind is required as part of the major turnaround in the mind, and this ability will train you in communication with others.

So start with Self, practising communication. This is a form of Self Love.

Start by saying something like this:

'I now openly express love to myself moment by moment, as I move to drop all limits that I have created for myself.'

Can you feel that as a true emotion when you say it?

Sit and say that to yourself.

'I am on a pathway to create the very best for me, Joy, Love, and a Peaceful Mind, by my actions, deeds, words, and thoughts.'

Sit and say that to yourself.

'I am Love itself.'

Sit and say that to yourself.

'I am in harmony and resonance with the grand mystery and intelligence that birthed me.'

At the 'moment interface of communication', at the moment when the words form, do you feel hesitation, do you feel connected? Does it feel hollow, and empty??

It is at this very moment that communication is formed.

Do you marvel at words pouring out of your body

mouth, moved by the Mind through to Body interface?

Where does this come from? It is so automatic. 'I can talk so easily!'

And what would you communicate?

That only Love is Real or… ?

At the 'Moment interface of communication', you will know whether you are or not.

Do you feel like biting your tongue off for what you said??

Would you like to try again?

Say this quietly to Self:

'I open myself to Reality Self and the grand intelligence that flows to and through this Self.'

Then say to the seemingly other person, or yourself:

'I would like to try this communication again, please.'

Step into the moment and allow loving communication to flow out of you.

'I am light itself, I am pure loving energy, I manifest that in my communication.'

If you feel that it is so, it is.

If you feel you would like to edit or have another try, do it.

As we said earlier, don't edit while you are preparing to talk or while you are talking. Allow these words to flow and then examine it and say, 'That was OK'.

or

'I can do far better if I step into my True Self and the emotion at the "Moment interface of communication" and speak with passion.'

You will know if you are being over the top and ridiculous and trying to impress.

And if you feel it came out all wrong or not clear or with no Love,

Say, Did you hear that?? May I say that again to you in a more loving way, please?

And then step into the moment and flow it out again.

Well done.

This is all feedback to you that you are able to flow Love out also.

Listen to your words.

Ask your friends or partner to comment on how you communication.

Listen to them and see if you can see that it is possible to move to a more open and loving means of communicating.

And so with that, we wish you all Joy, Peace of Mind, and Love flowing to you and through you.

Part II

In Dictionary Part I, we looked at a few words.

This may have been helpful.

This section we will look again, this time from Expectation onward.

Spirituality
Ego
Reality
World
Creation
Illusion
Insanity
Duality
Awareness

Consciousness
Time
Expectation
Mirror
Perception
Belief
Soul
Body
Matter
Spirit
Trans-formation
Trans-cendence
Trans-mutation
Effect
Cause

Expectation A hoped outcome, and even more, some outcome that may bring emotional effect if it doesn't come.

This is a word that may not serve well, as it is Ego-based and has the ability to cause Joy and Peace of Mind to drop or maybe disappear for a while.

What happens if your ego expectation is not attained?

Drop expectation for things on your terms, based on your will, and retain Reality and Peace of Mind.

Mirror This is one of these words for which very few, as of yet, have connected the dots.

The world is a mirror for you.

The world only ever mirrors back what you can perceive or believe.

If you feel or perceive that someone is threatening or offering help to you, it is only ever possible because that knowing or being able is in you or is part of your makeup.

A very good example:

If you love Jeshua, some would say Jesus, and say he is Christ, that can mean only one thing. You know and recognise this energy inside yourself also, and therefore you have these same qualities of Love in you, as he does.

He is a perfect mirror for your own Love and knowing Christ Mind.

And hence, the world you have created for yourself is your perfect mirror to heal yourself of misperception and belief that you have placed in it to see.

This is one of the major aha moments when you get this. Until then everything is outside of you and a threat or a blessing for you, with you as victim or victor. Either way you are in denial of your own mind.

Perception Much like Conception.

Perception is to bring to life the knowing (meaning and value) that flows to you from either Source self or Ego self, in each and every moment.

So mis-perception is to create from Ego false Knowing (meaning and value) in each and every moment. Ugh.

Belief Well, many say I believe this and that. Also I believe different than you.

Beliefs divide people one from another, to the point of being enemies with wars, strife, hatred, and bitterness.

Also it binds groups together as nations and causes the same thing internally, as it is a denial of reality in all respects.

Belief is a very poor attempt to replace Reality with a pseudo rule set.

At best it is Egoic and myopic.

See if dropping the word *belief* is possible for you.

You do not need to believe very much at all.

Each domain has its rules, it seems, for operation.

Spirituality always operates beyond these domain limits.

When you discuss your knowing and being with others, remove belief from the communication.

Soul A vehicle for experiencing individuation as Spirit, yes, a spiritual attribute.

All souls were created (or, more correctly, begotten) at the same time, when source replicated identical qualities of full self.

Body is fundamentally a projection of thoughts and ideas from Mind/s. A creation.

Therefore it can be said that body is surrounded by mind.

Same for Physical Universe.

A Body operates as a communication device (Jeshua) and a virtualised tool to give experience to a seemingly remote Mind.

Much like the remote-controlled surgical operator's hands.

Remote doesn't mean far away, just in another domain. You are never separated from Self in any domain.

Communication is established tri-directionally. The Mind in Reality, the biological creation as surgeon, and mechanical creation as hand. Three levels of communication it seems, to provide experience for the mind controlling the hand.

In this case, the experience is through two levels of virtualisation. Like a computer game.

Did you get that? The surgeon as a human biological body is not experiencing anything, neither the hand. It is still only the real Mind that is.

Matter A trick of Mind that was learnt a long time ago.

Converting light into matter. A trans-formation, a trans-mutation.

Maybe a big bang in consciousness??

Spirit is fundamentally energy, like the wind. Perceived but not seen in 3D Space and Time.

Intelligent Spirit is the one thing turning, the universe itself.

Trans-formation To change form.

Sadness to Happiness, from one energy form to another. A miracle.

Trans-cendence To overcome ego obstacles in the mind.

To let go and rise above, to a new awareness level.

Ascending up and over and down the other side of mental obstacles and energy, allowing Love to make the mental change.

A new you arises.

Possibly this example—

You have a mountain of energy in an Egoic Cause, blowing steam off as Effect, hissing and roaring everywhere in your life.

It can be said to be trans-cended when the creator of the cause (you) goes up one side of the energy and around it, inside it, and eventually stands on top and drives in his flag on the summit of the fear energy, exclaiming:

'I have released this energy mountain of fear with Love. It was my own creation and I can now move on to other mountains to conquer.'

A look back over the shoulder, with a smile and sometimes a little relief.

Trans-mutation To change energy levels of a certain form to a higher or lower level, by alchemy.

Lead to Gold >> Gold to Lead

Fear to Love >> Love to fear

Ego mind to Christ mind >> Christ mind to Ego mind

As you will be aware, this is only relative to non-reality, as you are always Gold, Love, and Christ in Reality.

So in Reality, trans-mutation is known as the last trick in the bag for the master magician.

A sleight of hand magic trick, a miracle, not understood by those stuck in body belief.

Keep practising the sleight of hand/mind until you are the magician of illusions, and when Master, then step across into Reality itself, leaving the magic bag behind.

Cause and Effect

You all know this by now.

Tell the person next to you right now.

For another understanding, read 601 again.

From your new understanding of taking responsibility, it makes perfect sense to move to your creations if you find you are having difficulty or pain with them.

Move to Effect.

It is your only window, gateway, or doorway to Cause.

This cannot be stressed more.

Healing comes from taking self-responsibility for creations and moving into the effect.

Embracing effect.

This is the divide between Ego and Spirit, right there.

The embrace of fear or effect.

It is only then that healing will come. Anything else is just window, gate, or door dressing.

Waste not another moment on window dressing, a brave face, a denial, a justification, a changing of the subject, a falling into victimhood once again.

We will leave the emotional words until next section.

This will be a fun section, as emotions seem to rule the waves of the ego consciousness soup.

However, they are excellent windows, gateways, and doorways for healing of the mind.

We are not done yet.

As always, I have been encouraged again to say more on communication.

This came to me when I was sitting quietly, and I had to get up and put it through the robot and the keys right away.

There are days coming when we will connect directly. We already do if you allow it, and you may be aware of this.

Some, to their surprise, are connecting to me regularly. I do know when you do.

And I love those moments when we share and heal emotions and pain seemingly remotely in human robot bodies.

Not really—it is only ever in our minds!

If someone loves you, that one will communicate with you, unseen and unheard by humans. Grow to know this. Open yourself to this.

Recently I was sitting quietly, and I had a realisation that I would like to share with all the minds moving towards harmony.

I have discussed this realisation with several since that quiet moment, and it seems a common set of habits.

So you seem to have made progress in dropping much re-activity and old habits, and life is easier. (aaaaahhh)

Gold stars on the forehead. Front of the class.

You are feeling freer and are now starting to look for more things to examine to make changes.

And then, here it is for you. Suddenly you become aware in one moment of an arising event in the mind that would talk to you.

Catch these types of moments.

You realise you have developed a new habit: blocking your ears so no one else can come into your bubble and talk to you. They cannot Communicate with you; you have limited availability.

or

If they do talk to you, you find yourself split, not wanting to ignore them but at the same time feeling a little annoyed that they are interrupting you from something very important (sitting quietly).

or

You may also notice that you are resisting old or new or other than acceptable information that arises, and you dismiss this information as nonsense.

Such as you find yourself saying stuff to someone or re-acting to politics, or religion, or eco or gender or culture or race or conspiracies or money or any blah,

Saying or thinking, this is all wrong (or right) and why doesn't everyone just let all that stuff go and get happy. Ohhh.

Hahaha. Yes, if you listen to your mind enough, it will be there, making a noise, keeping the whole place untidy.

You may even want people to join your petition or march with a placard to make it all right, your way. Oops.

This will arise for you one day when you are sitting quietly, and you will suddenly realise you are limiting yourself to a new pre-defined pattern of acting again rather than being open to all and any.

You have found a new comfort zone where you are right and they are all wrong. Oooops.

A new sabotage.

This arising is a simple thing to move through, of course, once realised.

Yes, some are smiling and saying, 'Oh my god, that is me. I have lost my vigilance!'

Ask yourself these types of questions:

Am I feeling superior now I am a spiritual master (and they are not)???? LOL

What is the limit I want to hold in place?

Is this limit serving me well?

Does it enhance communication?

Does it enhance relationship?

Does it drop Joy? Most importantly,

Does it cause a loss of Peace?

Does it cause constriction? (Loss of Love flowing to and through me.)

Does it arouse in me Christ mind? Oh no.

Ask what is cause around this swirl of effects.

And slip down into effect and move towards

cause—breathing with direction, to the energy that it is all wrapped in.

I open myself to the swirl.

I open myself to my own creations of swirl.

I desire to swirl with it completely now and sit in this swirl until I see the way to release this, so as to return to a much more Peaceful place.

I now open Myself to All Self (This is new—The One) to become available to all and every mind that wants to communicate with me, especially those that Love me.

And it is done with a sleight of hand.

A new creation of communication and broad inclusive relationship arises to be truly of help today.

Just by catching a background swirl in the mind, sitting quietly.

Play with this. Don't let a moment slip by.

These types of arising events are to be trusted and allowed and embraced; then trans-form, trans-cend, and trans-mute.

Get up and type or write them all down so as not to lose them.

Send me more to embrace.

Send me more to dance with.

Send me more to fly right with.

Send me more to trans-mute.

I invite all those who love me to communicate with me, not just by voice or Facebook or texting but with pure communication.

Test it out. Take note of the communication and then ask, 'who is this', and note it, and then ask that person later, 'Were you feeling and communicating with me at this time?'

You may be surprised.

Love to you all until next time.

Part III

For the third part of the dictionary, we will look at the last pieces and a couple of phrases that may not make a lot of sense at first:

You don't know what a single thing is and what it is for

and

There is nothing outside of you.

And then the host of words used in Ego talk that will need some further consideration as you move to a spiritual life.

A reconsideration of meaning and use of the words:

Guilt
Judgment
Fear
Separation
Vulnerable
Victim
Stuck
Denial
Anger
Confusion
Shock
Excessive Joy
Unresponsive
Disgust
Low Self-Esteem
Grief
Irritated
Resentful

And also some little word whiskers:

But

Should
Could—They will just drop away
Would
Because
If only

There is also a long list of sub words that spin off from the major emotion list, words that try to further capture the nuances of emotion and feelings.

The first phrase, *You don't know what a single thing is and what it is for.*

Answer >> How can an insane mind ever know what a single thing is and what it is for?

You may recognise and know names of objects, but what they are for and what relationship they would have with you would be mis-construed to fit that insanity. The communication would be limited, and what to do with things would be a lesson. Much like a beginner carpenter or a musician or an artist.

Relationships based on body-centric identification lead to a very limited view of self and everything else.

Next phrase: *There is nothing outside of you.*

Just how far do you want to take this discussion?

At first it may seem to be because everything is only ever experienced in the mind, and that is why there is nothing outside of you. >> Yes, it is a good start point.

How can a distant star not be outside of me? Ah yes, the body thing again. From a spiritual viewpoint, there is only one Reality, and creation (the star) is not it. Also, all creation is suspended and sustained by mind, with a thought (the star).

So it can be said that body issues from mind, that physical universe can be said to be suspended inside mind, in the thought, and it can be said wrapped as if in a swaddling blanket, surrounded by mind Loving it, nurturing it.

At Spirit level, physical creation is therefore small.

And finally, there is only the one, the one mind, the one reality, the one love sustaining it, and it encompasses all and ever, and you are that one. So how can there be anything outside you?

Phew, yes, this is how it is.

And now we move to the long list of emotional words, coined in Ego for Ego. There is a great need in ego to define all the various levels of suffering, victimhood, and drama possible.

All the various shades of re-activity that can be made and felt.

The grand list of how Love can be mutated to be all of this.

See how powerful we are.

This list is actually only a small master set of words needed in Ego life to describe the dis-ease.

In the intellectual world, the words are much bigger and far too complex for the average feeble minds like us to understand. (Smile.)

And humanity creates the dis-ease all to be true as master magicians again, skilfully practising and honing the ability to emote, be in drama, and be a victim or a victor.

There is, therefore, a need to change viewpoint and value on the emotional word list and all those associated with it, as a spiritual life unfolds for you.

None of these words are actually based on truth, and the conditions can be said to be unreal.

However, it doesn't lessen the effect in a mind or a body controlled by ego that is making it all true.

A good way to lessen value in these words is to confess to the emotional and physical condition when it arrives and say, 'And I am creating this right here, right now'. With a smile, if it will come, and a hearty laugh.

If you can't, your value is still high on the mis-perceived meaning inside the word.

Just confess, sit with it until you can see and feel that, 'Yes I am creating it, I must be pretty clever, and I can quite easily un-create and take value away from it and return to Peace. I am the master magician of the meanings. They come, they go, and I remain untouched and return to Joy and Peace always.'

Just move from the effect (the meaning in the word) to cause, hit the delete key, and it is done.

Here is another grand opportunity to watch, monitor, and be vigilant.

Watch the words, and if they come out and you catch yourself speaking Klingon—oops, ego talk—smile and say to those around you, 'Yes, I am speaking Klingon, ego words, and I will start again for you all'.

And then do it.

You see how this mirrors re-activity. Words reflect the state of the mind. Where you are sitting in viewpoint and perception.

That is why it is sometimes amazing to listen to songs you like, watch TV and movies, and in general talk and hear the ego projection through the words and then smile.

And so our dictionary was far more than anticipated, once again.

It wasn't just meanings, it has led to a new viewpoint.

Finally a little note on becoming a teacher of God.

You do not have to believe God exists (as a special body separated from you, as religions teach).

All that is required is a Loving viewpoint and words and actions that teach only Love is Real. That is God-you.

The dictionary section is your opportunity to look at your words and step into pure ownership of your life and communicate only words that sit inside that energy.

Play with it, make it interesting, be a little silly.

To finalise this section, a discussion has been going on now for some time in the Master's teaching group about some of these emotional words and how they affect relationships and communication.

It was decided that one of the predominant emotions in the ego world involves all forms of victimhood.

The word *aggrieved* seemed to convey the response many feel.

This is similar to being galled.

It sits between anger and low self-esteem.

And by the way, many of these feelings actually take on a body mimic in specific organs.

That is why when a feeling or re-activity is dropped, so too is the body mimic, and a physical healing occurs.

You will experience this, if you have not already.

It is not a miracle, it is just what happens when you play around with mind, energy, and bodies.

So being aggrieved is common.

Ask yourself this simple question: Do I feel aggrieved?

About my parents, my brothers and sisters, my relatives, my teachers, my lot in life, my status, my health, my finances, my partner, my children, my life, my spirituality.

If you find something, it is very easy to let go of it.

Say something like this: 'This aggrievement is entirely created and nurtured by me.'

Now that is a hoot.

It is actually impossible for this aggrievement to be true in Reality, and why would I want it to be true inside my creations also? Pow!

I am pure Spirit, I am free, I am loved, I am forever, I am part of the one grand thing with purpose, intelligence, and life.

Did you see in those words that this is how heaven comes to earth, bringing Love from Reality into your creations, in an earth somewhere?

Dropping aggrievement will change everything—relationships, communications, and of course word choices.

Go to the person you feel the aggrieving about and explain to them what you want to do, to drop this and instead Love them again.

What a lift; you will not be split anymore.

You are becoming a teacher for God, for Love,

teaching 'Only Love is Real', not just with the words, but actually living it and being it.

This has been a very good lead-in for our last section, which is about healing.

We will focus on not just the actual healing but the method used to help the letting go.

Because, my dear friends, 'You need do nothing, save heal that small part of your mind that is hurting and causing suffering still'.

All the rest is complete and OK right now.

You are Home already.

Communicate this with one another. Allow your life experience to heal you, trust now each day that everything arising is for you to use in healing, embrace life fully, and trans-form yourself into who you really are already.

Show that it is possible to trans-cend all events, and trans-mute all fear, guilt, and judgment back to Love itself.

How's the Viewpoint??
Well done.
Love to you all

Shamaré—The Guardian, the Protector, the Door Keeper, and the Gate Keeper

Spirituality and Healing

As we enter into the last section, Spirituality and Healing, a slight re-arrangement of the mind may be required to adapt to the new information that is coming to you this time.

People often get quite excited in anticipation about the notion of healing, as they almost immediately translate it to mean healing the body.

However, there is only one thing that can truly be healed, and that is the mind, as nothing else truly exists.

Remember, bodies as creations, which are un-real, emanate from the mind and are held together by thoughts in that mind.

This does mean that if the mind's connection to that body is removed, the body will cease to function as a creation and expire.

So this re-arrangement of the understanding of the word 'healing' will allow you to hold to Joy and Peace, even when in physical dis-tress or physical dis-ease.

And if you are in dis-tress physically, always be kind to yourself and take a multi-faceted approach to your healing.

Distress comes from the Latin *districtus,* which basically means a divided mind.

In other words, the focus in pure mind and true mind is distorted, and there is no clarity. Two things/thoughts/perceptions are running simultaneously.

In many cases, you will not jump to full mind healing in a few days, weeks, or sometimes years, or even a lifetime.

However, you can start the process right now. What is an incarnation or two to make progress!

So be gentle on your mind and realise you may still need support from body practitioners at some points along the way, if the dis-tress focus is body-centric.

Along this Spiritual pathway, I have found the carcasses of many so-called spiritual masters strewn about, having become shipwrecked on this one mis-perceived point.

The one common denominator that most of these masters thought would differentiate them from others in their quest for status as a spiritual master was to overcome all and every ailment of their physical body first, and also achieve the ability to heal other bodies.

Failing to accomplish this body-centric healing often leads many to a great loss of Joy and Peace of Mind, and then an overwhelming projection, with a fall into a dark hole of mis-perceived failure.

The projection often blames the teaching that 'Only Love is Real'. That it is not true and Love doesn't heal bodies.

Often these ones will continue their seeking again, after licking their mental ego wounds, falling into modality after modality, in their lost quest.

Back to the same valley path, trod oh so many times before, on so many other incarnations.

They took it all so seriously about being master that they lost simplicity, and with it, their Joy and Peace.

Their quest as so-called master was more important than Joy, Peace, and Love flowing to them and through them, from the very depth of them.

They forgot they are already complete in all ways, except for one fact, and that is their focus is body-centric ego identification and not Spirit-centred identification.

Be careful about this one point.

Being Master is not a certificate but the natural state.

Stay simple.

Focus on Spirit.

Love self and be compassionate with all others.

Fundamentally, a body can said to be totally innocent even if this body seems to be not as you would like it to be.

A body is as it is. Born innocent into time and space, with an incarnating mind deciding how it will be for that body, most of the time.

This is true, even for bodies that are imperfect at birth.

We will see later the influence a mind has on an innocent body.

So Love the body that seems to be yours. It is your only vehicle for physical experience in this domain.

Your own success in healing your mind (and maybe with the body following) will be a direct result of the level of your surrender into the depth of the infinite mystery arising in you at all moments.

By the way, the information above may shock some, as it seems to be contrary to the many stories floating around about saviours and healers.

Many of these healer stories are only written in their form to create a certain outcome or impression.

Jeshua tells us that some who were healed in front of him 2000 years ago sometimes reverted back to the original dis-ease after a few days or weeks.

Ponder that: does this information make sense? If a healed person drops once again into ego fear and guilt, will they undo all the healing they did for themselves??

So after that interesting preamble about healing, some riddles to begin our quest for Mind Healing.

So to the riddles.

#1

If you don't know you don't know

—yes, you don't know.

Most ego minds only see what it is in front of them and are totally unaware that there is much more happening around them. Even the seeing in front is distorted or mis-perceived.

They remain in the dream that they are body, and they are disconnected from source and seem trapped and are a victim.

Stuck without true knowledge, they are even unaware that they are the one they are awaiting on all this time. Imagine the seeming disconnect in mind. And we have all been there and know this.

When in that state of unknowing, there is no question of having to know anything more; it is as it is.

#2

If you know you don't know.

You are moving to awareness.

These Ego minds are now becoming aware of their mental state, and it may lead to opening to knowing and discovering self once again.

A wondering is starting to happen. 'Maybe there is more, but what is it?' A search begins.

How this is triggered is most wonderful!

A call from inside is answered finally and the process begins.

An awakening to your own call.

All will attain this, of course, at some point.

And not necessarily now and in your time frame, so remain compassionate, as others have waited on you.

#3

If you don't know, you know.

You are on the cusp of opening to true knowledge.

These Ego minds have passed the first hurdle of 'Knowing they seem to not know something'.

They are out of complete darkness and opening to self, with awareness.

If someone discusses that knowing this something else is possible with them, this may be all that is required to kick the awakening process for them into great allowance and surrender.

They may start to open to their own knowledge and awaken.

First of all being told about it or reading in books, and then finally realising the experience of self.

Curiosity about knowing Self may take over.

Many in this state will sometimes wait or stall—in a religion, a philosophy, a saving-the-earth cult, a do it right cult, maybe reading horoscopes for direction, or seeking divination or magic from outside themselves, waiting on signs and portents, hoping for answers to life's riddles.

The reading of many books and attending of many seminars and workshops usually follows.

Or a waiting for a whole lifetime in a belief and faith state, hoping at the end a saviour will come and fix them for being so good. Snatched from hell to heaven.

When all these pursuits run out of steam, they will ask for someone to come to them, and that someone arrives just in time, at the right time, themselves.

Then desire is fuelled with Intention, and the process of Allowing spirit to direct life slowly comes; and after much struggle or less, a surrender can be born, into a new viewpoint, a spirit viewpoint.

#4 Ahhhh

If you know, you know.

You have mastered surrender.

Into the grandest of all things, the mystery of all, infinitely broad as it is deep, and infinite in knowledge and wisdom.

These have moved from body-centric belief to realisation of Spirit.

They are free as a bird and can soar inside the one mind as master once again.

Did you like the little riddles?

Ponder on them.

Where are you sitting??

These little riddles carry most of the information about the varying degrees of ego mind limits that you will bump into many times along the way to awakening, as you progress in healing the mind and possibly the body.

And of course, just to put the ship on the correct course again, Spirituality 101 until now has been about healing the mind.

As mentioned previously, the body often mimics the mind's dis-eases and distresses, manifesting physical and emotional diseases.

This is metaphorical, of course. What else could you expect?

Everything outside Spirit is metaphorical. Ponder this also! It has to be.

A mimic is a metaphor for something similar but in a different domain or creation or outside Reality.

Later, we will see how this works.

Many would-be so-called body-centric healers will try to heal a physical body without first healing the mind, using modalities, -isms, -ologies, drugs, magic, or even resort to surgery and cutting out parts of the body that seem to have failed or become dis-eased organically; and this malady may even threaten the life of that body.

You don't know you don't know.

And hence you and the body-centric healers don't know, and you remain stuck in no knowledge, outside Peace and Joy or fleeting touches here and there, with some healings and many cases of only masking of mind symptoms (effects) as relief.

The biggest selling drugs are painkillers, whether legal or not.

These drugs are killing the effect which we now know is the window, doorway, and gateway to healing!

However, note this, that all healers get a certain

amount of healing taking place, due to the patient jumping to mental healing themselves, just with the prompting thought of the healer or the drug or the modality.

These are called placebos, even used and known by the practitioners themselves.

In all these cases, it is mind healing that is taking place at some level.

It also shows the superb power of the mind and that even unknowingly, people can heal rapidly when they desire it and then know it.

As a body is organic, it does require organic sustenance, and if this is missing no amount of mind healing will fix these types of things.

Group # 1—Not knowing you don't know.

This is the majority of humanity at present, in ego identification most of the time.

This is a situation in which the ego is making the personality/body seem as a victim to some unknown dis-ease or problem inside or outside them, which they feel is outside their sphere of influence or ability and hence they may not even be involved in this dis-ease process.

They are often told this also by practitioners, which enhances the belief pattern in victimhood.

They pass responsibility for this problem to another who seems to be far better qualified than themselves to heal them.

If you run into people in these situations and states, in most cases leave it alone, as it does not matter; not really, as they unknowingly remain as they were originally created to be, pure spirit, untouched by the body and ego mind dis-ease.

Their body may survive or not, but their spirit body and mind remains intact for another try, when a new incarnation may be offered or decided on.

Please do not get trapped in feelings of being sorry for this one or that one. You can, however, be Compassionate and Loving. Their path is as it is, and they remain safe at all times.

There is no point in letting their projection of unknowing affect your Joy or Peace. Wish them well, push some Loving energy to them, say something profound and move on. They will awaken to their own call at some point, just as you are awakening. All will. All are safe.

Some healers seem to be successful, as they believe their modality works.

However, after many years of doing this modality as a Group #1 or a Group #2, one day or progressively, their awareness opens for them that their healings have all along been moving people to release at the mind level first and hence the release to physical healing.

Usually these healers, as they mature, move rapidly into Group #3 and even Group #4 with this awareness.

They will continue to use their old modality, hanging out their shingle on the roadside or media, but now focused on Spirit-centric mind healing, knowing full well that only the patient can heal themselves.

The modality becomes only a method to get clients to come and open and trust at an ego and body level.

You may have tried some of these modalities. I did many times and even practised them myself.

In fact, my friends, if you get an overwhelming feeling you want to go and see a certain modality healer, please go. It will be a certain stepping stone for you.

What you truly need will come out for you at that time. A stepping stone in awareness.

These healers are intermediaries for ego to Spirit, knowingly or unknowingly; it doesn't really matter.

Nothing really matters, as we are discussing spirit which is not matter.

In fact that statement of going and doing what you feel you need to do applies to everything in your life.

Sit on the arising desires you feel for a while, squash them down, and then the really strong desires will push to the top of the heap.

Go do them; they are more stepping stones for you.

Take the brake off and experience.

All sorts of things will come along and up for you in your mind.

The right new people, new experiences, new resistance to know and heal, etc.

However, as we draw close to the end of our discussion at this time, we have bigger fish to fry than physical modalities.

We are in reach of end points in Spirituality 101 to 601 and Beyond.

And it is all about yourself and the healing of your

mind directly, with you as healer and director of the sessions.

By the way, trying to fix others can become an obsessive compulsion that may lead to losing sight of the prize of the upward call of true self, to new levels of mental ascension, as mentioned at the start.

So let go of this and move forward into your own healing, moment by moment.

Those who come to see you about healing, and they will—work with them, hold them so they can heal and shake their healing off and move on.

You did not heal them; they did it themselves, with you as support.

In Group #2, where knowing you don't know has arisen for you and healing begins—

This Group #2 is growing every day.

Many of the children being born arrive in their incarnation already a #2, and it will only take a small amount of life for them to move to #3.

If you have children, talk to them directly about these things. Don't mess about with trying to get them integrated into body-centric thinking.

This directness may be helpful for you too.

Maybe your children have come to help you and let you heal.

There is a grand evolution arising in many spirits that are dreamers.

Spirits incarnating have got stuck thinking/dreaming that they are primarily and only human, identifying with body as self.

Many are awakening and opening their minds and declaring:

'There must be a better way. I know I don't know the way out yet but I step into ownership of this unknowing and ask/call out for directions now.'

When you happen to find yourself in this state of knowing your unknowings, it often leads to inner personal questions, and a quest is formed and a pathway is set to opening to knowing.

With this decision to open to knowing, you can return to Peace and Joy once again, and often body and emotional dis-ease will actually disappear as the mind's dis-ease drops away gently.

Dropping dis-ease in mind often drops the metaphor mimic in the body.

Also, for those who seem to be born into or have a body that has developed difficulties: This doesn't mean Peace and Joy are any farther away from you than anyone else, just because your body doesn't suddenly change and heal back to so-called normal.

These issues of health may be a very old and deep mind issue.

Surrender is the only way out of this seemingly endless dilemma of distress.

We are all spirit and share and use the same mind.

Having a broken body doesn't change this.

Only mis-perception does this changing and leads to dis-ease in the mind, which is reflected in the body mimic.

You decide the state of your mind.

Having a body that doesn't seem able to be well, see, talk, even move, or has some other limits is only an experience inside a creation; and those entering into this experience are brave souls indeed.

It tests the mental resolve to stay in Joy and Peace in a seemingly trying incarnation or circumstance.

There are no victims, ever; it is impossible.

If the body doesn't seem to heal or miraculously grow another arm, this is no reason to lose Joy or Peace, as you are not the body.

This, however, is quite a mental step to make.

To maintain Joy and Peace in an incarnation with a physical and emotional body that seems to not fit to being normal, requires exactly that, what you came for, that or this experience.

Consider this well: it is your body life experience, it is your spiritual life, and you can choose in any circumstance to be Joy and Peace at all times with Love flowing to you and through you.

Each and every moment, it is your life, sit in and work it well.

Just consider this one point.

If you were to cut the so-called silver cord (your incarnation connection to a body, a good metaphor), your mind remains as it is.

Your thoughts and perceptions remain as they are.

You, the Spirit in dream, will usually now move from that incarnation into lower frequencies of regret, using thinking and feeling.

I didn't manage to heal or master that body in that incarnation.

So Peace and Joy on the other side of the veil is not manifested even when getting free of a broken body in regret.

This often leads to another incarnation attempt, to master body.

Again, a mis-perception is started and a chance to become aware inside the dream, to stop the dream and heal, is on the cards again.

I would like you to recall back in the early Spirituality Notes the discussion about:

'The Truth that will set you free'.

It introduced the thought that no other concept works or brings Peace of Mind and Joy.

Only the moving of mental attention to spirit and the reality that spirit resides in will work.

That changing of mental attention is what is bringing and allowing mental Peace and Joy to be had.

Love flows again.

Every other concept known leads to circular

thinking, no clarity, insanity, dis-ease, distress, confusion, disappointment, and victimhood.

It leads to being trapped in a circular world, with no windows, gateways, or doorways out.

So therefore make straight your path, break the circle. Very biblical!

Healing is all about flying right into the doorway of healing, flying into mental effects, finding mental cause, releasing and remaining as you always have been, pure Spirit.

Always dwelling and experiencing in the one mind, where the default energy of Love is flowing to all, where Peace and Joy is the only possibility.

Since this series began, many have contacted me to tell me their progress, their lack of progress or being stuck, cries of help; and some have made a journey to visit in body so we can be eyeball to eyeball, as it is said.

There is a common theme in almost everyone that has written, talked, or visited.

What has become clear is the predominant mind issue.

This common issue is actually the doorway and mirror for healing.

It is not the only mental dis-ease present; however, it does seem dominant.

All the manifestations of mind dis-ease of non-released resistances, of ego-locked attention of self-identification, seem to stem from similar mental beliefs, traumas, sabotages, patterns, or habits.

So instead of giving a series of stories of how this one or that one healed their mind, as I thought I was going to, I will offer an allegory that can be mapped over the top of almost all minds who have reported in.

It might map your mind also.

As a side note, though, I have to say that those who reported being healed of this or that, almost none of them can relate the details of their healing and the underlying issues.

It has become hazy with the passing of time what the dis-ease even was, as they have already almost forgotten about it and it seems not to exist anywhere any longer, in a tangible form to be accessed.

That is true healing, when all traces of mis-perception are gone.

Semi-miraculous you can say. Amazing the first few times.

So to the allegory.

It happened one day when I was walking with another, and we were talking away as we walked, and then the communication connection with that other suddenly was disconnected and I looked around to find them stopped, several paces behind me, standing trans-fixed, as they watched a young person fly by on a pretty little dragon, in slow motion with great ease and splendour.

I had not noticed the dragon, but they did immediately and stopped, dropped their attention from me, and stood open-mouthed.

'Oh my god' was heard.

(We will see these are entirely true words.)

After a few minutes had passed, the other broke the attention to the dragon and looked back at me with a face that showed sadness and puzzlement.

We continued on our way, and after a short distance the other suddenly changed the direction of the conversation, saying:

'I am getting a migraine headache and I can't see properly, it is clouding over and I have great pains developing in my head. My stomach is really queasy.'

We sat down and after a few minutes, I started to ask simple questions of the other, now in great pain and discomfort in body and showing signs of overwhelming emotions, even starting to show signs of body-mind dissociation with shutdown, numbing out mentally.

An overwhelm was developing.

'When did you first get migraines?'

Of course in the midst of the pain the answer was like this:

'I don't know, I don't remember. Stop talking to me, I am in pain here.'

A Not Knowing has arrived on the scene.

Next question to help them break attention from the pain and become observer:

'Did you have migraines when you were a child?'

'No' was quickly uttered.

See, there is Knowing in there somewhere.

Next question.

'Did they start when you were an adult?'

'No, before that'—snapped back.

Now time is starting to be broken into pieces of Knowing and Not Knowing.

'When you were a teenager, 16, 17, 18, 19??'

Tapping into their mind here.

'I remember when now. I was 16 or 17 when they started.'

They have found the time zone, and now for the Knowing...

'Ah very good. And what happened when you were that age?'

'I don't know. I don't remember. Stop talking to me, I am in pain here.'

Here we go again, a seeming dis-connect from the Knowing.

A guess question, or maybe an intuition question, or maybe another tapping into the other's mind question.

'Tell me about when you had your dragon taken.'

'Oh my god (there it is again). I remember now, when I lost my dragon, I started to get migraines; that is when it started. I didn't think I could live without it. I was scared of the future, I couldn't see a future without it. I only get them now when, Oh yes, when I see a dragon and remember my childhood loss of my lovely dragon.'

The Knowing is starting to flow again; Cause has been found.

'OK, well done, you are connected to the memory of this well now. You are at cause.'

Letting them sit for a while to integrate that Knowing again, I asked after a few minutes:

'Do you recognise that you are creating the migraines now and then and in between? That is the effect.'

'Yes I do, it is a reaction to that old memory; I can see that clearly now.'

So now into the embrace, trans-form, trans-cend, trans-mutation, release and the healing of the mind for that cause is done.

'Ask yourself this question: "Does this dragon memory (creation, memory cause) serve me well now, after all these many years?"'

'No.'

Pause.

'It doesn't serve me well. I forgive myself for believing I needed to hold onto that feeling of loss of my dragon for sooo long. I was afraid of moving on as a teenager. I made it take away my Peace and Joy for many years.'

'OK, so let's keep on walking now and see how you do.'

'Yes, the migraine is leaving now, my sight is clearing and the pain has reduced.'

A few minutes later it is all gone.

So here is a rundown on the process.

A mind has a memory, an unhealed memory (one that takes away Joy and Peace of Mind), locked in place, with a great amount of energy flowing to it to keep it alive and present.

This mind activity flows directly from soul consciousness and awareness, as a spirit in Reality.

This particular soul has an incarnation running in its mind also.

It is connected to a biological body form, a chemical, electro, light powered, very well designed robot body on a planet spinning somewhere in a virtual or created physical universe.

This incarnation in this soul's mind is running via a telemetry link from the Spirit's mind to this particular body in a created domain.

The comms link is highly intelligent and is fully integrated to all the systems in this biological body.

The soul via mind is able to power up and move this body, but more amazingly, the body can provide comms back of pictures, continuous movies, sound, touch, taste, etc. directly to the soul's mind in real time, to be analysed and deciphered, and then decisions on this body data arise in the soul of how to feel about it all.

This leads to emoting for the soul, now involved in virtual body experience with the remote robot body as so-called life.

The remoteness is not distance, as the soul is intimately linked to the body via a zillion connections.

The remoteness is about domains that are different between the body and the soul.

This soul has lost awareness that it is linked with a zillion connections to a body and sits in a dream, in an illusion, running itself on a mis-perceived identification that it is actually the body now.

That is how illusionary the link becomes. The confusion of which domain they exist in becomes overwhelming as body and ego develop.

With this particular incarnation, a decision was made earlier by soul that a certain event or experience needed to be underlined and highlighted as critical for this incarnation to become a healing time.

A full awakening this time, maybe.

In this allegory, when the dragon was seemingly lost by the body's eyes and the soul emoted about it, lamented about it, became victim about it, the experience got stuck in the soul's mind as a cause not to be forgotten but something to feed and react to every time a trigger came by to launch the cause in memory as re-gretful re-membrance.

In that incarnation, from then on, whenever dragons were seen an effect would arise and be generated in the soul's mind.

Once the soul's mind saw the dragon via the body's comm uplink, the soul's mind would feed back by the comms downlink to the robot. It would now project comms signals that made the robot's body change its electrochemical light status. A re-activity, an experience happens even in the body. Very, very clever.

The cells of this robot body would go crazy trying to follow the comms signals from the soul's remote mind.

In case of dragons, the body systems would almost become overloaded, and communication services in some cases could be lost to the robot if the robot got overwhelmed and collapsed.

If this happened, the body's biological eyes would start to shut down, the head would start to ache, the stomach would start to churn, and the hearing would change. This would all be fed back to the Soul's mind for processing and then further responses and feedback control.

The experience would be a closing in one.

This is the metaphor in full swing. The body is mirroring or mimicking the mind directly in real time.

And it is only an experience, an event, inside a dream because the remote mind linked directly through incarnation to this body has become self-identified with the body.

The soul is thinking it is the body and a victim. It is oh so real.

As the soul's mind feeds instructions to the body how to react, there is a feedback loop back to the mind, saying how it is all going at the body side.

The mind and biological overwhelm, the high emotions are generated as the signals back and forward get amplified or made bigger, so it becomes the full monty, the big hairy drama.

Don't you love this, and it is happening every moment multiplied by several billion continually.

A world inside worlds, inside worlds of creations.

So the mind is now going, 'oh my god, things are out of control here, it is getting worse', and the feedback can run away on itself in both directions, and the robot collapses.

A complete panic attack at each end of the comms connection.

Here is why the first thing that must be done in any healing is to get the spirit, the soul, into observer state.

Break or slow the comms feedback loop.

Break the attention.

Questions can do this.

A good master will know immediately that at some point, the soul in trouble will need to break attention to the effects going on.

This is why questions help it break attention.

This is why breath is so good as it breaks attention. A defocuser.

This is why a glass of water is good, better whisky you say, yes whisky. Haha

See how easy it is? And who has been using that for eons??

Everyone really knows the way to heal. (Keep the whisky handy.)

Get them into observer mode.

There is nothing happening here and all other cases, other than a spirit, a soul perceiving incorrectly, 180 degrees out of phase with Reality.

These sorts of happenings are very common to a spiritual teacher, almost minute by minute each day these sorts of scenarios arrive either directly in front of them or by remote connection; and they can be of help in those moments always.

Mis-perception running in a mind of a soul that is

in dream state, believing they are body, is all that is going on.

Nothing terminal here, just a glitch in perception.

A master walks up to anybody, acknowledges the spirit, the soul, and knows that there is nothing real wrong here, except mis-perception.

So ask yourself these questions now:

What is your dragon you lost when you transitioned from childhood to teenage life, or teenage to adult life, that seems to still have a hold on you?

Was it something tangible like the loss of a pet, a cat, dog, horse, or a friend?

Maybe a parent or a brother or sister was lost.

or

The dragon may have been your freedom to dream and play.

It was taken/lost as you were maybe forced to grow up and become what culture says you must be like as an adult body personality, fitting in this way and that.

Maybe you had to move locations, change schools and make new friends, or maybe you couldn't make friends, or maybe you were isolated and bullied.

Maybe you felt your dragon was lost when you weren't loved as a child anymore.

Maybe you were accused of something that was small but it became big for you.

Maybe you did something you felt was bad or wrong and you never forgave yourself.

Maybe it was sexual in nature and you were disturbed by this loss of innocence at a young age.

If it was a family member or relative that seemed to take the dragon away, there is often a strange mixture of trust and mis-trust that develops between family members, a type of poison for the whole family mind.

Let's pause here.

You can see this discussion is quite simplistic in nature, and it's just to make the point that each person often has an experience that seems to stick as an aggrievement from their childhood or youth.

A transitional moment with loss, something taken from you or a decision you regret.

A panic that things will never be innocent and simple again.

Accessing this lost dragon moment and letting it out often brings a rapid change in dis-ease in the mind, and in many cases in the physical and emotional body, such as the one discussed in the Allegory.

In the real case, this is exactly what happened and almost as quick and easy.

As I make a quick scan of all the people who are closest to me, I see all of them have lost a dragon at some point and are still upset by this at various levels.

It shows in their lives on and off over time.

It only comes up, of course, on a trigger, such as the allegory when a dragon flies by and the memory is stirred once more.

This is what has been discussed over the whole series, with each page of the Cause and Effect theme.

The easy access into the doorway, into Effect and then the Cause, such as in this story is sometimes not a simple five-minute communication.

A good master can usually get there quickly—with practice.

However, for someone working alone on their awakening, it can take many years of seemingly hunting under every park bench and inside every cupboard in the mind.

There may be better ways.

Find a good Master who has moved to point where only Love is Real for them.

That is why they are Master, of course!

Often two are better than one, but not always.

A good time is when alone in bed at night, between 1:00 and 5:00 a.m., sliding into the mind in a Peaceful state, to crawl around all the nooks and crannies, exploring, opening to knowing and entering into dialogue with true self and others that come along as support, and they do.

And now we enter into the meat of the discussion, to move from metaphor to true Self-Healing.

We will broaden this discussion out, to actual Full Cause and Effect, 601 again, with true mind healing and possibly body and emotional healing following along also.

We know that the existence of the physical world is billions of years, thanks to our very clever human robot scientists who love digging into such things.

Tell yourself what is incorrect about that??

And we have existed long before that, as we now know we are responsible for the physical universe coming into being, and also sustaining it at spirit level.

How many incarnations do you suspect you have had?

Many, would be a good guess.

How many dragon experiences have you had as a child?

Many, would be another good guess.

And of course the meat in this tasty sandwich is your first childhood experience.

First Cause and First Effect, as discussed in the 601 and Epilogue.

Cosmic Child losing a grand dragon it seemed, losing connection with true self, source of all things.

That dragon loss haunts all souls in incarnation as

humankind and many other domains, to this very moment.

How to heal it?

I remain as I was created to be, pure spirit, pure innocent cosmic child, loved always and safe in all circumstances.

That was quick, wasn't it? Right to the heart of the matter, in a few words or ideas—phew.

Break the mis-perception quickly.

Break the attention to loss and victim.

There is this very interesting story of Jeshua's return to Palestine from India when he was about thirty years old. He had been away for about thirteen years.

He was wondering what was next for him, and this story tells of his recovery from his lost dragon or from Cosmic Child loss, to being Christ again.

We are all Christ, as we know now. Even now, the ascension has happened, you just don't see it yet.

Just to say it once more. Christ means anointed or approved one.

Well, you are and no one can take that away from you except yourself.

He was sitting under his tree of course, out of the sun, when this idea arose into his mind. I suspect he was daydreaming, just kicked back lying there, with wine, maybe a few figs and dates.

If I can bring the start point (before my Dragon was lost) back into my mind as reference point, attention point, reality point, all will trans-form and heal.

He walked into the desert, pulled everything out of his dis-eased mind, all his dragons, his cosmic child and human child hurt, he emoted, wailed, and stomped around the sand and walked back out of that desert, once again in that innocent mental state that is mirrored in all reality to us.

A perfect reflection of self, un-hurt and with out dis-ease.

With out = Outside dis-ease

You can say—With out your dragon, with out. Kick it out the door of your life.

It all fell away progressively, headaches went, he could see again, the emotional fields healed, his mind cleared for him—until three years later he was so clear, he walked into the big experience to show that even body death is unreal.

And a nice final trick: made a new body and came

back as avatar and ran to the south of France with Mary and the children, ending up in Tibet later.

It was just like the other person in the migraine experience.

Just a walk along the road, a pause, a few questions, a few rememberings, the release, a healing, and another walk and talk.

A cosmic child suffers a trauma, losing their dragon. Later a trigger re-lights the memory of the original trauma, that now leads to a re-enactment of the first experience and they regenerate their migraine headache, loss of sight, and queasy stomach, the huge envelopment of their body with their generated emotional energy, a clouding-over of the mind, a loss of innocence, a fall into victim once again.

Lost in creation!

As soon as the cause was found (a stolen dragon) and released—and this does take a remembrance and an ownership of that creation, that it hurt to lose the dragon, and they generated the hurt—then the decision can be made to release it, in Love.

It is just changing the perceived value of the first or original experience.

Did I really need to make it so painful?

It doesn't seem so important anymore. Breathe in, breathe out, smile and heal. Love flows to you and through you from the depth of you fully now.

Ego makes minds sticky for dragon stories, to find a place to hang them.

Note: Pure Innocent Spirit can have a dragon experience, and laugh and drop it and move on, un-touched, un-sticky always. (I release you.)

It is the being serious that makes it sticky.

So examine your dragons hanging on the wall around you, and release them if you choose.

You may like some of these as stuffed pets still, and you can't let them go yet.

Eventually you have to let them all be free again.

Stories abound of people healing the mind, and their life radically changes forever.

Don't get too envious of these stories. Make your own story of freedom and a return to innocence.

Be Master. You are already, you are just shy and hide it away. (Bushel baskets again.)

In fact you already have changed radically since you started reading these pages.

You are not the same as before. How could you remain the same, knowing what you know now?

You now know you know,

or

are very close to allowing that #4 Riddle to be so for you.

Take a very deep breath in and declare:

How could it really be any other way.

Impossible, only in dreams.

And laugh heartily.

Well done; it has been a long journey, many words, many ideas.

Contemplate these over again and again until they take root in your heart again.

Be prepared at any moment to change again and again, evolving and shifting mental shapes and perceptions over and over.

There is much to change and release and find and release again, to find again and to change again.

En-Joy the hell out of your life (a little Jeshua funny—he likes that stuff).

We are the ones bringing heaven to earth, with all of this. All over the globe, the ones that know that 'Only Love is Real' are growing in power and numbers each day. Many in our original group of several hundred now share these messages with friends. You may do so also.

And finally, my dear long-suffering friends, yes you have put up with all of this so well. Not one complaint from anyone, amazing! Maybe you are all sleeping!

You are about to be commandeered also by spirit.

Each of you will eventually become teacher, too, so start early. Don't wait for another incarnation.

If there is resistance to this, take a breath, become observer by moving into feeling, into effect, down into cause.

'Oh, please stop it, we have heard that a thousand times now', you will say.

Oh yes you have, and please don't you forget it.

Teach it to others.

Teach them that love allows, trusts, embraces, trans-forms, trans-cends, trans-mutes all things.

Teach them that they are all in truth, pure Spirit, and remain as they were created to be.

Nothing has changed except for a short dream that they aren't spirit.

Tell them they are loved always, and are forever and always part of the one thing, never to be separated, always in communion with and are part of this one loving thing.

Everyone, every soul is brother or sister (actual without gender), no chance of anything else.

Encourage them to move into every moment as a healing moment, embracing their creations for healing.

Tell them nothing is outside of them, and that everything they see is a reflection of their own perception running. Life is a mirror only.

They are not victims, they are creators and just seemed to have got trapped inside some of their creations for a short while.

No one has ever done anything to them; they have created all outcomes and responses.

A party awaits their awakening.

Heaven on earth is their mantra, even if they do not have a body to participate in it when it reaches full fruition or expression.

I will probably be asked to say some more things at some point. I do feel many of you, as you struggle with various causes and effects.

You can talk to me about this if you like.

It may be a dragon release that is required, as a small embryonic spirit child feeling first effects from the one cause.

A simple five minute walk and talk, a breath in, and a breath out.

The way is easy, the load is light, now that you have found your new Viewpoint to sit in.

'I am Spirit, I am Loved always, I am always.'

Therefore, may you find the Peace and Joy you seek.

It is waiting for you, as you open yourself to allowing that Love to flow to you and through you always, not from a source apart from you, but yes, from the very depth of you.

Yes, that Self Love makes all the difference. It is the Source of your natural Joy and Peace always.

And as that Love flows to you, allow it out to others, no matter where you find yourself and no matter what form you be at that moment.

Love Healing all things, as only Love is Real.

How's the Viewpoint now??
Well done until we meet again.
Love to you all

Shamaré—The Guardian, the Protector, the Door Keeper, and the Gate Keeper

About the Author

Shamaré lives in remote hills in Northland, New Zealand surrounded by forests, birds, animals, streams and nature. From an early age, he knew that the world he was being shown was missing some essential knowledge. This knowledge, as spiritual writings from Shamaré, has been shared worldwide to a private group of friends for more than 20 years.

His commission now is to bring this knowledge to mainstream readers worldwide, to share a vision of the future where humanity can finally bring heaven to earth as a reality. Shamaré (designated as the Guardian, Door Keeper, Gate Keeper and Protector) is now a public instructor of this knowledge and is available to meet your group of friends to share and expand this knowledge.

Shamaré's teachings may very well become the opening and support you need in your own pathway to awakening fully.

www.shamare.com

www.ingramcontent.com/pod-product-compliance
Lightning Source LLC
LaVergne TN
LVHW021652060526
838200LV00050B/2312